USING CHATGPT AS A WRITER'S ASSISTANT

Unlocking Creative Potential with AI

STEPHEN HAUNTS

Copyright © 2023 Stephen Haunts
Published by Adventures in Writing. A brand of Stephen Haunts Ltd

https://www.adventuresinwriting.com/

All rights reserved. No part of this book may be reproduced or used in any manner without the prior written permission of the copyright owner,
except for the use of brief quotations in a book review.

Developmental / copy editing, and proofreading by Scribendi

Manuscript version 1.0

To request permissions, contact the publisher at www.adventuresinwriting.com/contact

Paperback: 978-1-7394213-4-2
Ebook: 978-1-7394213-3-5

This book is dedicated to my wife Amanda, and my children Amy and Daniel.

About the Author

Stephen Haunts is a writer who lives in Derbyshire in the United Kingdom with his wife and two children. Stephen and his family are fans of theme-parks and rollercoasters. He's happiest when hanging upside down, and hurtling along a rollercoaster track at 100kph, or sitting at his desk writing novels.

twitter.com/stephenhaunts
instagram.com/stevehaunts

Also by stephen haunts

STEPHEN HAUNTS

On Writing Your First Novel: The Journey of a Wannabe Novelist is a guide from Stephen Haunts, an experienced nonfiction author turned novelist, exploring the in-depth journey of crafting a debut novel and preparing it for publication, offering first-time authors indispensable advice to navigate the world of novel-writing.

Also by stephen haunts

Between football games and bullies, living on Mars seems a lot like living on Earth. That is, until twelve-year-old Elliot makes a discovery that may hold the key to one of humanity's biggest questions: Are we alone in the universe?

Contents

Introduction	11
1. CHATGPT AS A WRITING ASSISTANT	**41**
ChatGPT as a Thesaurus for Evocative Writing	44
ChatGPT To Help with Research	50
ChatGPT To Suggest Names	58
ChatGPT To Write Poetry and Lyrics	66
ChatGPT To Simplify Text or Expand Text	71
ChatGPT To Brainstorm Story Ideas and Outlines	77
ChatGPT To Rephrase Text	90
ChatGPT To Study Book Outlines	95
2. CHATGPT AS A MARKETING ASSISTANT	**106**
Writing Blurbs is Hard	108
ChatGPT to Write a Blurb for Diary of a Martian	112
ChatGPT to Write a Blurb for Little Red Riding Hood	124
3. IN CONCLUSION: EMBRACING THE FUTURE OF WRITING WITH CHATGPT	**135**
Please Leave a Review	138
Also by stephen haunts	139
Also by stephen haunts	141

Introduction

In the evolving landscape of artificial intelligence (AI), there's a robust and creative force that has been transforming the way we communicate, learn, create, and write. This force, a sophisticated language model known as ChatGPT, has emerged as an indispensable tool for writers, offering a plethora of writing help that transcends conventional methods. *Using ChatGPT as a Writer's Assistant* is a guide that unveils the immense potential of this innovative technology and how it can be harnessed to bolster your writing prowess, regardless of your niche.

The essence of this book lies in its detailed exploration of the many ways that ChatGPT can facilitate and enhance the writing process. ChatGPT is not just a thesaurus, offering synonyms and antonyms at your command, but also a resourceful research assistant that

Introduction

can provide you with valuable information on a wide range of topics. Are you struggling with naming a character or a place in your story? ChatGPT can suggest a multitude of names tailored to your specific context.

However, the scope of this AI's capabilities does not stop at the conventional aspects of writing. It delves deeper, venturing into the realms of poetry and lyrics, offering you help in crafting rhythmic lines that convey your unique voice. It's an adaptable tool, capable of simplifying complex narratives or expanding on ideas, providing you with the flexibility to mould your text following your needs. With the realm of fiction also well within its purview, it can present a whirlwind of story ideas for those times when you're grappling with writer's block.

As you navigate further into this book, you will also explore a unique facet of writing that often proves challenging for many – marketing text. The art of persuasive writing, which encompasses blurbs, log lines, tag lines, and promotional text, requires a distinctive approach that can be quite disparate from writing a novel. ChatGPT, with its ability to generate an array of marketing text, can help you master this skill. Whether it's crafting compelling ad copy, intriguing tweets, or a sales text that resonates with your target audience, this book will guide you on using ChatGPT to enhance your marketing communication.

Introduction

Using ChatGPT as a Writer's Assistant strives to empower writers by leveraging the capabilities of AI. This book is a testament not just to the strides made in technology but to the human spirit of creativity, which seeks innovative ways to express and communicate. By exploring the intricacies of using ChatGPT as a writing aid, I hope to inspire and assist writers in their journey of crafting captivating narratives, powerful poetry, and persuasive marketing text. Welcome to a new era of writing, one in which AI serves as a catalyst for human creativity.

Introduction

The History of Technological Fear and the Promise of AI

From the dawn of civilisation, innovation has been a double-edged sword. It brings with it the promise of progress, yet it's frequently met with fear and resistance. Today, as we stand on the cusp of the AI revolution, it's worth looking back at how society has reacted to previous technological innovations, and what lessons we might glean for the future.

The Looming Looms: The Industrial Revolution

The Industrial Revolution of the eighteenth and nineteenth centuries transformed society in ways previously unimaginable, but it also sparked widespread fear. The most iconic of these fears was the Luddite movement, in which groups of disgruntled textile workers in England, threatened by automated looms, took to destroying these machines in protest. They feared that this new technology would lead to unemployment and the devaluation of their skills. The opposite was true, and automated looms ushered in a new era of innovation, and employment, utilising and developing new skills for workers.

The "Pencil of Nature": The Advent of Photography

When photography was introduced in the nineteenth century, it was met with both awe and anxiety. Many artists feared that this new medium would render their skills obsolete. After all, why spend hours creating a portrait when a camera could capture an image in seconds? Yet, over time, artists adapted, using photography as a tool to aid their work or even incorporating it into their artistic expression.

The Digital Dawn: The Arrival of Computers

Fast forward to the twentieth century, and the advent of computers triggered a similar reaction. Many feared that these "electronic brains" would replace human workers, leading to widespread unemployment. While computers did automate many tasks, they also created new jobs and industries that hadn't existed before. They became tools that enhanced human productivity, rather than replacing humans outright.

The AI Conundrum: ChatGPT and Beyond

Today, we face a similar crossroads with AI and, in particular, AI language models like ChatGPT. There's a genuine fear that these technologies will replace writers, journalists, customer service agents, and more. It's true that AI has the potential to automate certain tasks, but it's essential to remember the lessons from history.

Like the looms of the Industrial Revolution, the cameras of the nineteenth century, and the computers of the twentieth century, AI is a tool – a powerful one, but a tool nonetheless. Its purpose is not to replace humans but to augment our abilities.

ChatGPT, for instance, can generate human-like text, but it doesn't possess human creativity, experiences, or emotions. It can't craft a compelling narrative or a touching poem with the depth and nuance that a human writer can. What it can do is assist in the writing process, helping us to overcome writer's block, brainstorm ideas, or draft initial copies that a human can then refine.

Innovation as Opportunity

Fear of technological change is a natural human reaction. However, history has shown us that innovation often leads to progress and new opportunities. The key is not to resist change but to learn how to adapt and make the most of it.

With AI, this means grasping how to work with tools like ChatGPT. It means understanding its strengths and limitations and figuring out how it can enhance our skills rather than replace them. It's an opportunity to redefine roles and find new ways to express creativity.

We shouldn't fear innovation. After all, the introduction of automated looms didn't take away jobs—it created a new industry, photography didn't kill art, and computers didn't eliminate work. These tools changed their respective landscapes, yes, but they also created new opportunities for those willing to adapt. As we stand on the brink of the AI revolution, let's not cower in fear of the unknown but instead welcome the opportunities it presents. This change is not about being replaced; it's about adapting and evolving. It's about working with new tools to create, express, and achieve like never before.

Introduction

What is ChatGPT?

In a world where technology and AI have permeated every sphere of our lives, a novel invention is sparking a revolution in the realm of writing. That invention is ChatGPT, a language model developed by OpenAI. But what is ChatGPT, and how does it work? How is it transforming the world of writing?

At its core, ChatGPT is a sophisticated AI program that understands and generates human-like text. It's trained on a vast array of internet text, but it's not just regurgitating what it's seen before. Instead, it generates unique responses based on the context it's given, making it an interactive tool that can assist in various writing tasks.

How does it work, you ask? Well, ChatGPT employs a deep learning model known as the Transformer, which uses machine-learning algorithms to predict the next word in a sentence. It learns patterns in the data it's trained on, helping it understand context, sentiment, and nuances in language. But don't fret if this sounds overly technical – all you need to know is that ChatGPT draws information from a massive amount of data to generate coherent, contextually appropriate responses.

Now, let's talk about how ChatGPT can be a game changer for writers. Imagine having a writing assistant

Introduction

that never sleeps, doesn't ask for breaks, and is ready to help whenever you need. That's ChatGPT for you.

Human-like Thesaurus: Struggling to find the perfect word or phrase? ChatGPT can act as a thesaurus, suggesting alternatives that can enrich your writing. It can offer synonyms, antonyms, and related phrases based on your text's context.

Research Aid: Need quick information on a topic? ChatGPT can provide summaries, descriptions, or explanations, saving you time on preliminary research.

Name Generator: Looking for a name for a character in your novel or a title for your next blog post? ChatGPT can come up with creative suggestions.

Poetry and Lyrics Assistant: Writing poetry or lyrics? ChatGPT can help generate rhythmic lines or even complete verses.

Text Simplification or Expansion: Looking to reduce or add text? ChatGPT can help simplify complex language for better understanding or expand on ideas when you need more detail.

Story Brainstorming: Stuck with writer's block? ChatGPT can offer a range of story ideas or even help develop plots based on your preferences.

Where ChatGPT really shines is in the world of marketing text – an area that requires a distinct skill set.

It can help generate compelling blurbs, catchy tag lines, persuasive sales text, promotional tweets, and engaging ad copy. This AI tool can be a secret weapon for writers looking to master the art of persuasive writing.

ChatGPT is an AI-powered writing assistant that's here to transform how we write. It's not here to supplant us but to enhance our abilities, helping us overcome challenges and expand our creative horizons. So whether you're an established author, an aspiring writer, or someone who just wants to express themselves more effectively, ChatGPT is a tool worth exploring.

Introduction

Decoding the ChatGPT Language Models: Differences Between GPT-3, GPT-3.5, and GPT-4

In the realm of AI, the evolution of OpenAI's language models has been nothing short of transformative. From their initial iterations to the latest advancements, these models, particularly the generative pre-trained transformers (GPT), have been continually pushing the boundaries of what AI can accomplish in natural language understanding and generation. Let's delve into three significant milestones in this journey – GPT-3, GPT-3.5, and GPT-4 – and explore how each version differs from the other.

GPT-3: A Leap Forward in Language Understanding

When GPT-3 was unveiled, it marked a significant leap in AI. With a whopping 175 billion parameters (parameters are the parts of the model that are learned from historical training data), GPT-3 demonstrated an unprecedented ability to generate human-like text. It could write essays, answer questions, translate languages, and even create poetry. However, despite its vast capabilities, GPT-3 had limitations. It could sometimes produce incorrect or nonsensical answers and had a tendency to be excessively verbose. It had no memory of past requests, making context-heavy conversations challenging.

GPT-3.5: A Step Towards Better Interactivity

GPT-3.5 served as an intermediate update, aiming to address some limitations of GPT-3. It provided improvements in managing dialogue-based tasks by maintaining a more coherent context during a conversation. It also incorporated fixes to reduce verbosity, resulting in more concise responses. However, while GPT-3.5 offered enhanced interactivity, it didn't fully address certain issues, such as producing incorrect or nonsensical responses.

GPT-4: The New Frontier of Language AI

GPT-4, the latest version at the time of writing, has introduced significant advancements over its predecessors. Although OpenAI has not officially disclosed specific technical details and the number of parameters for GPT-4, the improvements are noticeable. It exhibits enhanced abilities in understanding and maintaining conversational context over longer periods, making it more useful for in-depth dialogues. It shows improvements in generating more accurate and meaningful responses.

GPT-4 has a better handling of potential misuse and biases in the model's responses. It has been trained with methods to refuse output that could be potentially harmful or misleading, ensuring a safer interaction with the AI. It is worth noting, however, that no model is perfect, and users should know the potential for errors or biases in AI-generated content.

The progression from GPT-3 to GPT-4 represents a journey of continual learning and improvement, with each version bringing its own set of advancements and challenges. These models have significantly expanded the capabilities of AI in understanding and generating human language, offering immense potential for various applications, from writing help to customer support and beyond.

As we embrace the potential of these powerful communication tools, with each new version becoming more sophisticated, nuanced, and effective, it's crucial to understand their limitations and use them responsibly. However, the journey doesn't end here. As we look forward to future iterations, we can expect OpenAI to continue refining and expanding the capabilities of its language models, pushing the boundaries of what's possible with AI.

Introduction

Understanding ChatGPT Prompts

In the world of AI, the term "prompt" holds significant value. When interacting with OpenAI's language model, ChatGPT, a prompt is the input you provide to the AI, which it uses to generate a response. Understanding how to craft effective prompts is crucial for getting the most out of ChatGPT.

What are ChatGPT Prompts?

A prompt can be anything from a single word to a complex sentence or a series of sentences. It could be a question, a statement, a command, or a creative scenario. Essentially, it's the information you provide to ChatGPT to guide its response.

For instance, if you're writing a science fiction story and need help brainstorming ideas, your prompt might be something like, "Generate five unique concepts for a science fiction novel set in the year 3000." The AI will then produce a response based on the prompt, providing you with a series of ideas. Or, you may be struggling to think of a new name for some bizarre alien technology; everything you come up with just doesn't sound right. You could ask ChatGPT "Generate names for an alien technology that uses force fields."

Why Are Prompts Important?

Prompts are the steering wheel for navigating a conversation with ChatGPT. The AI uses the prompt to understand what you're asking for and to guide its response. The quality and clarity of your prompt directly influence the relevance, accuracy, and usefulness of the AI's output.

A well-crafted prompt that clearly states what you want can often result in highly effective results. For example, if you want to use ChatGPT as a thesaurus, a specific prompt like, "Provide synonyms for the word 'happy'" will yield a concise and useful list.

How to Craft Effective Prompts

Crafting effective prompts is an art in itself and often requires practice and experimentation. Here are a few tips to get you started:

Be Specific: The more specific your prompt, the more likely you are to get a useful response. ChatGPT does not have a deep understanding of your thoughts or context beyond what you provide in the prompt, so detail is crucial.

Provide Context: If your request requires understanding a particular scenario, include that context in your prompt. For example, if you're asking for character dialogue in a story, provide some background about the character and the situation.

Experiment: Don't be afraid to try different prompts to see how the AI responds. Sometimes rephrasing a question or providing additional context can dramatically improve the output.

Prompts are the cornerstone of effective interaction with ChatGPT. By understanding what prompts are and how to use them effectively, you can unlock the full potential of this powerful tool, whether you're using it for writing assistance, research, brainstorming, or any other creative endeavour. Remember, effective prompts lead to effective responses.

Introduction

The Ethics of using Generative AI

As the capabilities of AI continue to evolve, so too does the potential for these technologies to shape and influence our world. Generative AI, like ChatGPT, stands at the forefront of this transformation. Offering a versatile tool for writers, it can generate text that is human-like in its sophistication and nuance. However, as when using any powerful technology, it is important to understand and address the associated ethical considerations.

Authorship and Originality

One of the first ethical issues to consider is the question of authorship. If a piece of content is generated by an AI, who owns the work? Is it the developer who trained the AI, the user who provided the input, or perhaps even the AI itself? These are complex questions without straightforward answers, and they highlight the need for clear guidelines regarding the authorship of AI-generated content.

Closely related to the issue of authorship is originality. As AI becomes more sophisticated, the line between human creativity and AI-generated content can become blurred. It's crucial to maintain the distinction between human-authored and AI-assisted content to ensure the value and recognition of original human creativity.

Bias and Fairness

AI systems, including ChatGPT, learn from the data they are trained on, which often includes biases present in our society. These systems can inadvertently generate text that perpetuates stereotypes or displays unfair biases. While OpenAI has made significant strides in mitigating these issues, writers need to remain aware of this and take steps to avoid perpetuating harmful prejudices and assumptions in their own work. Don't always take facts generated by ChatGPT at face value; be prepared to fact check important facts for accuracy.

Privacy and Confidentiality

Generative AI models like ChatGPT do not have access to personal data about individuals unless it has been shared with them in the course of a conversation. They generate responses based on patterns and information they've learned during their training. However, as AI evolves, so does the potential for misuse. Writers must be mindful of this and ensure that they do not inadvertently disclose sensitive information while using these tools.

Misinformation and Disinformation

The ability of AI to generate realistic, human-like text also carries the risk that it could be used to spread misinformation or disinformation. While AI can be a powerful tool for creativity, it could also be exploited to create false narratives or misleading content. It is crucial for writers to use AI responsibly, fact-check AI-generated content, and make sure their work does not contribute to the spread of misinformation.

As we explore the potential of generative AI, like ChatGPT, we should navigate these ethical considerations thoughtfully. As writers, we are uniquely positioned to shape narratives and influence perceptions. With this power comes responsibility. Using AI tools ethically means acknowledging their limitations, understanding their implications, and striving for transparency, fairness, and respect for the value of human creativity.

It's an exciting time to be a writer in the era of AI. Used thoughtfully and ethically, tools like ChatGPT can help us push the boundaries of creativity and reach new heights in our writing endeavours.

Introduction

Embracing ChatGPT as a Writer's Assistant, Not a Replacement

It's understandable that many are wary of how AI might change the face of our creative pursuits. As a writer, I've watched the development of ChatGPT with interest, even awe, and have formed my own views on how this tool fits into the writing process.

The essence of writing, particularly the crafting of a novel, is inherently human. It's a mosaic of our experiences, thoughts, emotions, and creative imagination. It's hours upon hours of dedication – bum on the seat, fingers on the keyboard, and navigating the seas of creativity. I staunchly believe that this process, as traditional as it is, should not and cannot be entirely replaced by AI.

However, this doesn't mean that we should shun AI technologies like ChatGPT. We can embrace them, not as replacements, but as invaluable assistants in our writing journey.

ChatGPT, in my view, is revolutionary. It's like having a writing partner who's available 24/7, ready to help whenever you hit a roadblock.

Nevertheless, I wouldn't use ChatGPT to write the actual text of a novel, at least not yet. Partly, this is because I believe the heart of a story should come from a human. But there are also practical considerations. For instance, questions surrounding the copyright of AI-generated text are still not fully resolved and need to be tested in court.

New technology, particularly something as transformative as AI, can be intimidating. It forces us to question our roles and the value of our skills in a changing world. However, rather than resisting change, I believe we should learn to adapt and find ways to make these advancements work for us.

The rise of AI doesn't signal the end of human creativity; instead, it offers us new tools to explore and express that creativity. As writers, we can harness the power of technologies like ChatGPT to help us break through barriers, generate new ideas, and enrich our storytelling.

In the end, the story is ours to tell. AI is just another tool in our kit, and how we use it is up to us. For now, I'll keep my bum on the seat, my fingers on the keyboard, and ChatGPT by my side, ready to assist whenever I need a spark of inspiration.

ChatGPT and the Importance of Fact-Checking

As we integrate AI into our daily lives, it's essential to understand how to use these tools effectively and responsibly. ChatGPT has become a popular assistant for a range of tasks, including research. However, while ChatGPT can provide a wealth of information, it's not infallible. Here's why you should always fact-check the information it provides.

ChatGPT: A Helpful, but Not Infallible, Tool

ChatGPT, like all AI models, generates responses based on patterns it learned during its training. It has been trained on a vast range of sources, including books, websites, and other texts. While this diverse training enables it to generate responses on a wide variety of topics, it also means it can propagate inaccuracies present in its training data.

Furthermore, ChatGPT doesn't have the ability to access real-time information or databases to verify facts as it's not connected to the internet. It doesn't "know" information in the same way humans do; it generates responses one word at a time based on patterns from data it was trained with, not verified truth.

The Importance of Fact-Checking

Because of these limitations, information provided

by ChatGPT shouldn't be taken at face value, especially for critical or high-stakes research, and should always be cross-verified with reliable sources. Here's why fact-checking is so important:

Accuracy: While ChatGPT often provides correct information, it can occasionally produce inaccuracies or outdated information. Fact-checking ensures that the information you're using is accurate and up-to-date.

Context: AI models like ChatGPT can sometimes miss nuances or context that are obvious to human readers. Fact-checking can help ensure that you're interpreting the information correctly and in the right context.

Reliability: By fact-checking, you establish the reliability of the information. This is especially crucial if you're using the information for something important, like an academic paper, a news article, or a business decision.

How to Fact-Check Effectively

When fact-checking information provided by ChatGPT, here are a few steps you can follow:

Check Multiple Sources: Don't rely on a single source for verification. Look for multiple reputable sources that confirm the information.

Use Reliable Sources: Make sure the sources

you're using are trustworthy. These could be academic journals, reputable news outlets, official websites, or expert-authored books.

Stay Updated: Especially for topics that change rapidly (like technology or current events), ensure the information is up-to-date.

ChatGPT is a powerful tool for generating ideas, drafting text, and conducting initial research. However, it's not a definitive source of facts. Be sure to use it responsibly by fact-checking its responses, ensuring the accuracy and reliability of the information you use. This way, you can make the most of what AI tools like ChatGPT have to offer without falling into potential pitfalls.

Introduction

Using This Book

I designed this book as a guide to assist writers in leveraging the potential of ChatGPT as a writing tool. Each chapter is devoted to a particular area of writing, such as brainstorming ideas, simplifying or expanding text, writing poetry and lyrics, and crafting marketing text.

The chapters are structured to provide practical, hands-on experience with ChatGPT. Each section within a chapter presents a series of prompts that you can use with ChatGPT, along with examples of the AI's responses. These prompts and responses serve as a starting point, demonstrating how ChatGPT can assist in various writing tasks. Here's how to get the most out of this book:

Study the Prompts: Understand the structure and context of the prompts provided in each section. I carefully crafted these prompts to elicit specific responses from ChatGPT.

Analyse the Responses: Look at the responses generated by ChatGPT. Note the accuracy, relevance, creativity, and any potential biases or inconsistencies.

Understand the Discussion: Pay close attention to the discussions that follow each prompt–response example. These sections provide valuable insights into how the AI model operates and how it can be guided to produce better results.

Experiment: Use the prompts as a starting point to interact with ChatGPT. Experiment with different prompts and variations to see how the AI responds.

Reflect and Hone: Based on your experiences and the discussions in this book, refine your approach to using ChatGPT. Develop your own best practices for interacting with the AI model.

I do not intend this book to provide a definitive way to use ChatGPT. Instead, it offers guidance and strategies based on my own experiences and explorations. The true potential of ChatGPT as a writing assistant lies in your hands, and how you choose to wield this powerful tool is up to you. Happy writing!

Introduction

Accessing ChatGPT

ChatGPT is easy to use. Follow these basic steps to get started on the AI tool yourself.

Visit the Platform

Navigate to the ChatGPT interface at chat.openai.com or any other platform that hosts the model.

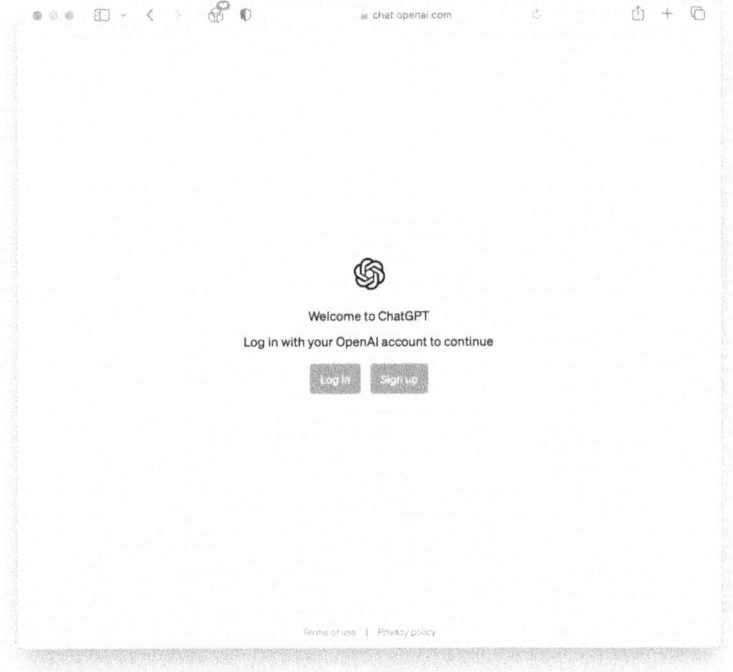

Sign Up / Log In

If it's your first time using the platform, you'll likely need to create an account. Look for a "Sign Up" or "Register" button, and follow the prompts. If you already have an account, simply "Log In".

Familiarise Yourself with the Interface

Once you're logged in, you'll see a chat interface. Here, you'll interact with ChatGPT much like you would with a human via instant messaging.

Start Chatting

You communicate with ChatGPT by typing in your prompts or queries, and the AI will respond. ChatGPT's responses depend on the prompts you input. The more specific and context-rich your prompts, the more likely you are to receive a useful response.

Introduction

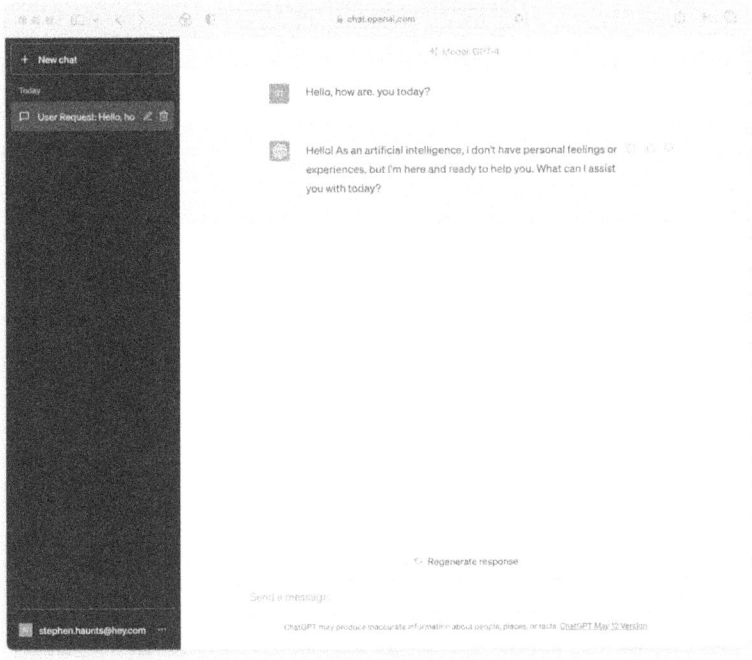

Note: For the most current and detailed instructions, always refer to the platform's official documentation or user guides. AI is a rapidly evolving field, and procedures can change frequently.

ONE

ChatGPT as a Writing Assistant

In the landscape of technological advancements, the emergence of AI has opened up new frontiers of possibility. One such frontier is the realm of writing, where AI tools like ChatGPT have been making waves. This chapter delves into the fascinating potential of this AI model in assisting writers in their craft.

Writing, whether it's a novel, a poem, a screenplay, or marketing copy, is an intricate process. It requires creativity, research skills, a firm command of language, and, often, a good deal of patience. Along the way, writers can encounter various challenges, from writer's block to the need for meticulous research or the struggle to find the perfect word or phrase.

Enter ChatGPT, an AI language model developed by

OpenAI, which has shown remarkable capabilities in understanding and generating human-like text. But what does this mean for writers? Can a machine really assist in a task as inherently human as writing?

This chapter explores the many ways in which ChatGPT can serve as a writer's assistant. It can act as an ever-ready brainstorming partner, a thesaurus that offers an array of synonyms, a research assistant that provides a starting point for deeper investigation, and even a co-lyricist in song writing or poetry.

While AI is not without its limitations and should not be seen as a replacement for human creativity or critical thinking, it's a tool that offers immense potential. We'll dive into how to use ChatGPT effectively, harnessing its strengths and mitigating its weaknesses.

The aim of this chapter is not to advocate for AI-authored literature but to explore how AI, specifically ChatGPT, can be a valuable assistant to writers. We will navigate through several practical applications, supported by real examples and insights.

So, whether you're a seasoned writer, an aspiring author, or someone who writes for professional or personal purposes, this exploration of ChatGPT as a writer's assistant aims to equip you with another tool for your creative arsenal. Let's delve into the world where technology meets creativity and discover how AI can be a part of the writing journey. I will present a series of prompts given to ChatGPT and include the AI's output with no modification, so you can see exactly what it generated.

ChatGPT as a Thesaurus for Evocative Writing

The first example I want to look at is using ChatGPT as a simple thesaurus. All you need to do is ask it to suggest alternatives for a word. In the following example, the prompt asks for an alternative to the word "punish". You'll notice that I also give context for the word's usage.

PROMPT: I need a better word than "punish" when talking about telling off a child in a story.

REPLY: Instead of using the word "punish" when describing the act of reprimanding or scolding a child in a story, you can consider the following alternatives, depending on the tone and context you desire:

Reprimand

Scold

Discipline

Correct

Chastise

Lecture

Rebuke

Reproach

Remonstrate

Admonish

Choose the word that best suits the specific situation and the atmosphere you wish to convey in your story.

In the reply, you can see ChatGPT's suggestions, which include various alternative words that fit the requested context. Looking through that list, I quite like "chastise" as an alternative, so I can now ask ChatGPT to use that word in an example sentence in relation to telling off a child.

PROMPT: Can you give me an example, using the word "chastise", when telling off a child?

REPLY: Certainly! Here's an example of using the word "chastise" when telling off a child in a story:

With a stern gaze, the parent leaned forward, their voice filled with disappointment and authority. "I must chastise you for your thoughtless actions," they said firmly, their tone conveying a mixture of concern and reprimand. The child's eyes widened, aware of the gravity of their mistake as the weight of the words settled upon them.

The response ChatGPT gives is helpful, and this feature is more useful than using a traditional thesaurus as you can see the word in use in a piece of prose. Let's try another example with the word "rebuke".

PROMPT: Can you give me an example, using the word "rebuke", when telling off a child?

REPLY: Certainly! Here's an example of using the word "rebuke" when telling off a child in a story:

The parent's voice pierced the air, sharp and resolute, as they rebuked the child for their reckless behavior. "I must rebuke you for your careless actions," they declared, their words carrying a sting of disapproval. The child's shoulders slumped, feeling the weight of their wrongdoing under the weight of the stern rebuke.

As before, ChatGPT provides an example of that word in a sentence. Notice that it uses the word three times, twice as a verb (the word rebuke itself and the past tense "rebuked.") and once as a noun ("stern rebuke").

Pushing the AI's capabilities further, in the next example, instead of creating a sentence using a word, we take a simple phrase and ask ChatGPT to rewrite it in a distinct style.

> **PROMPT**: I have a line in a story, "And then the rain poured down. Striking the ground with force." Can you write that in a more provocative and emotive way? I want a sense of dread as the rain falls.
>
> **REPLY**: The heavens unleashed their fury, releasing an onslaught of raindrops that descended upon the earth with a relentless intensity, their impact upon the ground reverberating like an ominous symphony of despair.

The response certainly is more provocative and emotive, and drips with atmosphere, especially the "ground reverberating like an ominous symphony of despair".

Let's try again, but, this time, we'll ask ChatGPT to write the phrase again in a darker and more sinister tone.

> **PROMPT**: Can you give me another version that is darker and more sinister?

> **REPLY**: In an unholy descent, the heavens tore asunder, spewing forth a deluge of malevolence. The raindrops, no longer mere droplets, materialized as harbingers of doom, pummeling the earth with a ruthless force that echoed the wails of the damned. A sinister dance ensued, as each strike upon the ground unleashed a chilling whisper, a foreboding melody that echoed through the very core of existence.

The response certainly fulfils the requirement of the prompt. It's a bit of a mouthful, but you could go further and ask ChatGPT to keep the same style but simplify the vocabulary.

Let's try one more example, this time rewriting the original phrase, "And then the rain poured down. Striking the ground with force," in a more romantic style.

> **PROMPT**: Can you write another version that is more romantic?

> **REPLY**: In a breathtaking display of nature's passion, the heavens opened up, bestowing upon the earth a cascade of liquid kisses. The raindrops, like ethereal

lovers, descended with tender grace, their gentle touch upon the ground igniting an enchanting symphony of desire. Each droplet, infused with the essence of longing, caressed the earth's surface, leaving a trail of glistening ardor in its wake. In this passionate downpour, hearts danced to the rhythm of nature's amorous embrace.

Well, romantic it certainly is. As an exercise for you, the reader, how about asking ChatGPT to try an action and adventure style? As these examples show, ChatGPT has a way with words, from acting as a simple thesaurus to rewriting phrases in a particular style. ChatGPT also works well as a dictionary, so if you want to know the meaning of a word, just ask. Let's now look at using ChatGPT as an assistant for research.

ChatGPT To Help with Research

ChatGPT is a useful tool to help you with research, and it's much more immediately useful than using a search engine like Google. While Google is powerful, it doesn't really give you a straight answer; instead, it will give you a list of sites to wade through. ChatGPT is more direct.

Remember though, that you mustn't take everything ChatGPT tells you at face value as it can make mistakes. The GPT 4 language model has improved in this regard, but it can still get facts wrong. So, as you work your way through your research, fact-check and cross-reference the answers that ChatGPT provides. This is no different from the practice of a journalist or researcher for a TV show; they will always cross-reference information with other sources to check its validity. It is no different with ChatGPT.

Let's start with a very simple closed question and see what we get. A closed question is a question for which you expect a yes or no answer.

PROMPT: Did humans and dinosaurs exist on Earth at the same time?

REPLY: No, humans and dinosaurs did not exist on Earth at the same time. Dinosaurs went extinct around

65 million years ago, while the earliest known hominin species, which are ancestral to humans, emerged around 6-7 million years ago. This means there was a significant gap of time between the extinction of dinosaurs and the appearance of early humans.

The answer is no, but ChatGPT tries to be helpful and gives you some context for the answer. A better style of prompt is an open question, which typically results in a more detailed answer, as in the following example.

PROMPT: Is there any documented evidence of alien on Earth?

REPLY: As of my last knowledge update in September 2021, there is no widely accepted scientific evidence or documentation of aliens visiting or interacting with Earth. Despite numerous claims and anecdotes of encounters, abductions, and sightings, no conclusive, verifiable evidence has been presented to support the existence of extraterrestrial life visiting our planet. The search for extraterrestrial life, however, continues through scientific endeavors such as the search for microbial life on other celestial bodies within our own solar system and the exploration of exoplanets in distant star systems. It is always important to critically evaluate the sources and credibility of any claims regarding extraordinary events or phenomena.

That's an interesting reply, but I already know about the "supposed" crash landing of a UFO at Roswell, New Mexico, so we can probe further and ask for more information. It is important to recall that ChatGPT has an awareness of the entire conversation, so you are not asking a question from scratch every time. ChatGPT can remember what came before your new question, which makes it good for a long-running conversation.

PROMPT: What about Roswell?

REPLY: The Roswell incident is a famous case often associated with claims of an alleged UFO crash near Roswell, New Mexico, in 1947. According to the initial military reports, a "flying disc" had been recovered, but the subsequent official explanation stated that the object was a weather balloon. This discrepancy between initial reports and the official explanation has led to various conspiracy theories and speculation about a government cover-up of an extraterrestrial event.

However, it is important to note that multiple investigations, including those conducted by the U.S. Air Force, have concluded that the wreckage was, in fact, a top-secret project called Project Mogul, which aimed to monitor Soviet nuclear tests using high-altitude balloons. The Roswell incident is widely regarded by the scientific community as a case of misidentification or confusion, rather than evidence of extraterrestrial visitation.

While Roswell remains a topic of interest and controversy, no conclusive evidence supporting the existence of aliens or an extraterrestrial spacecraft has been presented in connection with the incident.

The response we get when asking about Roswell is relatively detailed and contains many interesting facts, especially around the weather balloon. Let's just go ahead and ask about the weather balloon and see what it comes back with.

PROMPT: Tell me more about the weather balloon at Roswell?

REPLY: In the context of the Roswell incident, the weather balloon explanation refers to the official government statement provided in 1947 regarding the recovered debris near Roswell, New Mexico. Initially, the U.S. military issued a press release stating that they had recovered a "flying disc," but later revised the statement, asserting that the debris was, in fact, part of a weather balloon.

According to the revised explanation, the debris was associated with a top-secret project called Project Mogul. This project was developed to monitor Soviet nuclear tests by using high-altitude balloons equipped with special listening devices called sonobuoys. These sonobuoys were designed to detect acoustic signals generated by nuclear detonations in the upper atmosphere.

The Project Mogul balloons were made of neoprene and carried a train of instruments and radar reflectors attached by cables. The combination of the debris materials and the presence of the radar reflectors led to initial confusion and speculation about the nature of the recovered wreckage.

The explanation put forth by the U.S. military in 1947 was that the debris found near Roswell was from one of the Project Mogul balloons, which had crashed to the ground. They asserted that the "flying disc" description in the initial press release was a result of misidentification.

It is important to note that subsequent investigations and research, including those conducted by the U.S. Air Force, have supported the Project Mogul explanation for the Roswell incident. They concluded that the debris was consistent with materials used in the Project Mogul balloons and that the event was a case of misidentification rather than extraterrestrial visitation.

However, despite the explanations provided, the Roswell incident has remained a subject of interest and controversy, with various conspiracy theories suggesting alternative explanations involving extraterrestrial spacecraft. The debate continues, but the prevailing scientific consensus maintains that the incident was related to a terrestrial weather balloon project rather than an encounter with alien life.

Again, the reply includes numerous interesting facts, and from here, you could dig in deeper, for example, by asking about Project Mogul. While we are discussing aliens, let's see what ChatGPT can tell us about Area-51 because it's interesting and fun, and ChatGPT lets you jump down many curious rabbit holes.

PROMPT: Are there Aliens at Area-51?

REPLY: The existence of aliens at Area 51 is a topic of speculation and conspiracy theories. Area 51 is a highly classified United States Air Force facility located in the Nevada desert. It has been associated with UFO sightings and claims of extraterrestrial activities.

The U.S. government officially acknowledges the existence of Area 51, but its primary purpose is related to classified aircraft development and testing. It is believed to have played a significant role in the development and testing of experimental aircraft and advanced military technology.

Regarding the presence of aliens at Area 51, there is no credible scientific evidence or official confirmation to support such claims. The overwhelming majority of UFO-related claims or reports lack substantial evidence and are often based on personal anecdotes, speculation, or misinformation.

It is important to approach claims about aliens or extraterrestrial activities with critical thinking and rely on credible scientific sources for information. While the idea of alien life is fascinating, the current scientific consensus is that there is no conclusive evidence to prove the existence of extraterrestrial beings visiting Earth or being housed at secretive facilities like Area 51.

I wasn't expecting to receive a definitive answer about something that is probably highly classified, but the response was useful. As you can see, ChatGPT is an excellent tool for conducting research for your story ideas. Be warned, though; it can be a lot of fun. You might find yourself spending hours and hours asking questions and diving deeper into your chosen areas.

If, for example, you are writing a mystery, ChatGPT can help you come up with a crime and then design suspects and their motivations, means, and opportunities for committing those crimes.

Let's now look at another area ChatGPT can help with – coming up with names. This can be the bane of any novelist's life, but at least ChatGPT has no shortage of ideas.

ChatGPT To Suggest Names

Coming up with names for characters, places, or planets can be a real challenge for any writer. Every time I try to do it, I feel as though the names are very cliched or just don't feel right. Luckily, ChatGPT is good at this task.

For the first example, I am going to go a little out-of-this-world as this is something I have had to wrestle with as a science fiction author. (I'll go more earthbound later in the chapter.)

> **PROMPT**: Can you suggest some names for an alien species?
>
> **REPLY**: Certainly! Here are some suggestions for names of alien species:
>
> Xerendians
>
> Quasarids
>
> Nebulons
>
> Celestians
>
> Zephyrians
>
> Lumarians
>
> Draconians
>
> Epsilonites
>
> Orionites
>
> Aquilianthropes

Vortexians

Galaxians

Stellarians

Andromedans

Cosmarians

Feel free to mix and match, modify, or combine these names to create unique and intriguing names for your alien species in your story or creative work.

As you can see, ChatGPT gives you an extensive selection. If you don't like any of the names, you can click the button to regenerate the answer, which will offer a different list. Out of these names, I quite like "Nebulons". Let's now ask ChatGPT to come up with names for aliens that live on the planet Nebulon.

PROMPT: Can you suggest some alien names for the Nebulons?

REPLY: Certainly! Here are some alien names for the Nebulons:

Zyraxis

Luminara

Astronis

Nebulox

Quasarix

Stellara

Vortexia

Galactron

Lumisar

Orionis

Cosmonyx

Novastra

Zephyrion

Celestrix

Nebulae

Feel free to choose or modify any of these names to suit your preferences and create a unique and captivating identity for the Nebulon aliens in your story.

Again, we get a broad selection of names, so if I need a cast of aliens who live on the planet Nebulon, I have numerous options. I rather like Luminara, Quasarix, Vortexia, and Novastra, in case you were wondering. I appreciate that not everyone enjoys science fiction, so let's step back onto 1920s planet Earth and generate some names.

PROMPT: Can you suggest some posh sounding British names for a story set in the 1920s?

REPLY: Certainly! Here are some posh sounding British names that would suit a story set in the 1920s:

Algernon Pembroke
Beatrice Whitworth
Cedric Montague
Delilah Astor
Edmund Worthington
Felicity Fairchild
Geoffrey Kingsley
Harriet Channing
Ignatius Sinclair
Josephine Kensington
Lucius Fitzwilliam
Matilda Harrington
Nathaniel Ashcroft
Olivia Beaumont
Percival Radcliffe
Rosalind Somerset
Sebastian St. John
Theodora Cavendish
Vincent Townsend
Winifred Hargrave

Remember, these names are fictional and intended to have a posh and aristocratic feel that aligns with the

1920s British setting. Feel free to mix and match or modify them as per your story's needs.

I asked for posh, and that is certainly what I got. I can imagine my heroine detective, Beatrice Whitworth, running around solving crimes. My antagonist could be Lucius Fitzwilliam. That's a noble name. These names do sound posh, but I think we can go better and double-barrel the surnames.

PROMPT: Can you try again but with double-barrelled surnames?

REPLY: Certainly! Here are some posh sounding British names with double-barrelled surnames for a 1920s setting:

    Arabella Fitzroy-Smythe
    Benedict Worthington-Gresham
    Cecilia Montague-Sinclair
    Daphne Ashcroft-Harrington
    Edmund Beaumont-Channing
    Felicity Cavendish-Montgomery
    George Kensington-Winthrop
    Henrietta St. John-Winthrop
    Isabella Radcliffe-Harrington
    Julian Pembroke-Somerset

Lavinia Astor-Townsend

Maximilian Sinclair-Harrington

Octavia Kingsley-Fitzwilliam

Penelope Townsend-Channing

Reginald Harrington-Fitzroy

Seraphina Whitworth-Sinclair

Theodore Worthington-Ashcroft

Victoria Beaumont-Somerset

William Fitzwilliam-Cavendish

Xanthe Astor-Kensington

These names combine two surnames to create a more aristocratic and sophisticated sound. Feel free to adapt and modify them to suit your story and characters.

That's more like it. How about a story starring Daphne Ashcroft-Harrington or Reginald Harrington-Fitzroy? I must say, I'm tempted to write a 1920s cosy mystery with names like these. Now we have a great cast of British characters, we need a fictional English town for them to live in.

PROMPT: Can you come up with a list of fictional town names in England?

REPLY: Certainly! Here's a list of fictional town names in England:

Amberwick

Brambleton

Cheshireford

Daleshire

Eldermoor

Foxborough

Grayswood

Harlington

Ivybridge

Kingsbridge

Langford

Marlowe

Oakham

Pendleton

Quainton

Rosebury

Somerby

Tanglewood

Uptonshire

Willowbrook

These names evoke a sense of charm and idyllic English towns. Feel free to mix and match or modify them to suit your fictional world.

These names certainly fit the bill. However, when doing anything like this, it's always a good idea to search for the names, one a site like Google Maps. It is quite possible that some of these names already exist in England as we have a lot of strange names for towns. It's always best to check if you want an original name. Now that we have explored using ChatGPT to come up with names, let's look at generating poetry and songs that you can use in your novels.

ChatGPT To Write Poetry and Lyrics

Sometimes your story might require a poem or song, which can be hard to write. In the sequel to my novel, *Diary of a Martian*, I need one of my alien characters to take part in a poetry recital. It is a light-hearted part of the story. Let's start by asking ChatGPT to write a poem that sounds like a cross between the Klingon from Star Trek and the Vogon poetry from *The Hitchhiker's Guide to the Galaxy*.

PROMPT: Can you write an alien-sounding poem in a strange language that is a similar style to Klingon? It needs to be quite awful, like the Vogon poetry from The Hitchhiker's Guide to the Galaxy.

REPLY: On zyxalor's dread wings, flaxen tendrils intertwine,
 Vorpal essences entwined, where cosmic mysteries entwine.
 Llyzenthrala, snaq'reen's bane, a twist of primal melody,
 Dornakratyr, klaxen's blight, echoes of an ancient harmony.
 Uth'nor'gathor, snaar'gha's spawn, amidst the cosmic assault.

Tik'thorith, the endless maelstrom, devours the aeon's luminescence,

Sk'laathar, nefarious starbeast, feasts upon ethereal presence.

The response is certainly strange, but it has a major problem. In between the alien words, snippets of English appeared, which is not what I wanted. To get around this, I prompt ChatGPT again, specifying that I want no English words or phrases.

PROMPT: Can you write again, but with no English words or phrases?

REPLY: Vyl'koshan tor'gul, thraxian sk'laru entwyrn,

Vorpalan shal'zir, xenthroqian vyrn'kal urn.

Llyzenthrala, snaq'reen'shan bane, vranthar'lexan melor,

Dornakratyr, klaxen'shan blight, rith'zar eldor haror.

Ar'zhran zythal, flen'var shan uithaz melar,

Uth'nor'gathor, snaar'gha'shan, vaq'rish zentar kelar.

The result is better, but there are still a few English words dotted around, so I will just take the result and remove them myself. It can also be fun to ask ChatGPT to write lyrics for songs. In the following example, I deliberately give it a silly set of requirements, but it does a good job considering the obscure prompt.

> **PROMPT**: Can you write an annoying children's song about robots that like cheese?
>
> **REPLY**: (Verse 1)
> Zap! Zap! Clang! Clang!
> Robots marching, let us hang!
> They're made of metal, shiny and bright,
> With circuits buzzing, they're a curious sight.
> (Chorus)
> Robots love cheese, oh, it's their delight,
> From Swiss to Cheddar, they munch all night.
> Wheels of cheese, their favorite treat,
> Robots and cheese, a perfect feat!
> (Verse 2)
> Beep! Beep! Whirr! Whirr!
> Robots dance, don't you stir!
> Their gears are turning, oh, so fast,
> As they munch on cheese, it's a blast!
> (Chorus)

Robots love cheese, oh, it's their delight,

From Mozzarella to Gouda, they take a big bite.

Blocks of cheese, their joy and glee,

Robots and cheese, a tasty spree!

(Bridge)

Click! Click! Crunch! Crunch!

Robots snacking, they've got a hunch,

That cheese is yummy, a savory treat,

They gobble it up, it can't be beat!

(Chorus)

Robots love cheese, oh, it's their delight,

From Brie to Colby, they take a big bite.

Slices of cheese, they savor each piece,

Robots and cheese, a scrumptious feast!

(Verse 3)

Boop! Boop! Bzzt! Bzzt!

Robots giggling, don't you miss

Their cheesy antics, so much fun,

With circuits humming, the party's begun.

(Chorus)

Robots love cheese, oh, it's their delight,

From Blue to Camembert, they take a big bite.

Shreds of cheese, they sprinkle with glee,

Robots and cheese, a tasty spree!

(Outro)

Zap! Zap! Clang! Clang!

Robots marching, let us hang!

> They love their cheese, it's plain to see,
> Oh, robots and cheese, a jolly harmony!

It's a silly example, but it highlights just how powerful this tool is. You can easily ask ChatGPT to write poems or lyrics about any subject and in any format. Why not a poem in free-verse, a sonnet or a haiku? I encourage you to experiment with it. Let's now use ChatGPT for a much more utilitarian task – simplifying or expanding text.

ChatGPT To Simplify Text or Expand Text

ChatGPT is very helpful in simplifying or expanding on text you provide in a prompt. You may have a passage in your novel that is a little wordy. In that case, help is at hand. In the first example, I have a passage that is unwieldy, and I ask ChatGPT to simplify it.

> **PROMPT**: Can you simplify the following text: "This is a rather complicated piece of text that I decided to write about ChatGPT. ChatGPT is very good at helping to unknot incredibly complicated blocks of words and phrases and produce something that is quite delightful. If only I had the skill to be able to write as clearly, and this rather fantastic and brilliant piece of intelligent software."
>
> **REPLY**: I wrote a complex text about ChatGPT. It's great at untangling difficult words and making them enjoyable. I wish I could write as clearly as this fantastic software.

The response is certainly much clearer. It is important to stress that the answers given will not always be perfect, and you may need to refine your prompts with ChatGPT or take the result and tweak it yourself. In the next example, I want ChatGPT to expand some text. I have a very basic story, written as if created by a five-year-old, which I ask ChatGPT to expand with an advanced vocabulary. My request is quite vague, so let's see what it comes up with.

> **PROMPT**: Can you expand this story for children to 100 words using more advanced vocabulary: "Today it was raining. I wanted to go on a picnic. It was too wet. Instead, I ate my sandwiches at home. My friend came for lunch. Then, we played games."

> **REPLY**: On this eventful day, a gentle drizzle enveloped the world in a misty embrace. My heart brimmed with the longing for an enchanting picnic amidst nature's embrace. Alas, the raindrops persisted, rendering the lush meadows too saturated for exploration. Resolute in my desires, I adapted my plans and transformed my cozy abode into a culinary haven. With relish, I devoured my delectable sandwiches, their flavors dancing upon my tongue. Serendipitously, my dear friend arrived, their presence lending an air of joviality. Nourished and buoyed by companionship, we embarked on a joyful expedition of games,

laughter filling the air as raindrops tapped on the windowpane.

ChatGPT really had some fun with that. We went from a story by a five-year-old to a verbose mouthful. You can, of course, prompt ChatGPT to refine the result. Let's ask ChatGPT to rewrite this example as a horror story. I had to limit it to one hundred words for this example as my first attempt was over six hundred words.

PROMPT: Can you rewrite it as a 100-word horror story?

REPLY: On that fateful day, as the heavens wept, I ventured into the sinister embrace of a forbidden picnic. The rain-soaked earth whispered secrets of impending doom, yet I pressed on, driven by an insatiable curiosity. Alone, I devoured my sandwiches, their taste tainted by an unexplainable dread. A sudden knock shattered the eerie silence. My heart skipped a beat as my friend entered, a stranger with hollow eyes. A chilling air enveloped us, suffocating joy and replacing it with terror. We played games, but their twisted rules concealed a sinister agenda. That day, innocence faded, consumed by the darkness within.

ChatGPT certainly delivered. From a few short sentences that a young child could have written, it has created something spooky and foreboding. Let's throw this example on its head and ask the AI to rewrite it as a comedy – the polar opposite of a horror.

PROMPT: Can you rewrite it as a 100-word comedy story?

REPLY: On this comically ill-fated day, raindrops descended upon the world, as if the heavens decided to pull a mischievous prank. My grand plans for a picturesque picnic were drenched, quite literally, by this watery comedy act. Undeterred, I devoured my sandwiches in the absurd safety of my home, the rain's relentless pitter-patter providing a peculiar background score. Suddenly, a friend burst through the door, resembling a soggy clown. Laughter erupted amidst the deluge as we engaged in hilarious banter and slapstick mishaps. Our games took on a whimsical tone, defying the dreary weather with uproarious laughter. Truly, it was a day where even rain couldn't dampen our spirits, but rather added a touch of farcical charm.

This didn't exactly make me laugh, but it was an interesting attempt. With some additional prompting to include jokes or gags you find amusing, you could mould this into something funny. Still, this comedy is quite long and wordy. Let's ask ChatGPT to simplify the story for a six-year-old.

> **PROMPT**: Can you simplify for children, aged 6?
>
> **REPLY**: On this funny day, rain fell from the sky like a silly prank. I wanted to go on a picnic, but the rain made everything too wet. So, I decided to eat my sandwiches at home instead. Then, a friend came over for lunch, all wet and giggly. We played silly games and laughed a lot. The rain made everything seem extra funny, like a big joke. We had so much fun that day, and the rain couldn't stop us from having a wonderful time together!

That's not a terrible attempt. From here, you could copy that text into your story and alter it to fit your desired goal. It's unlikely that ChatGPT will give you something you consider perfect the first time. You will need to keep tweaking your prompts and letting the software try again. I rarely take finished text from ChatGPT; the text will always need editing and moulding to fit what you are working on. Let's now look at some examples of using ChatGPT to brainstorm ideas.

ChatGPT To Brainstorm Story Ideas and Outlines

I find that being a writer can be a very solitary occupation. I have other writer friends, but I can't spend all day talking to them and brainstorming ideas as they are also busy writing. ChatGPT makes for a great writing partner you can throw ideas around with. Let's try out some story ideas, and see what we can come up with. As I love science fiction, I am going to start there, but you can experiment with any genre that you like. I'm first going to ask for ideas for an alien invasion story.

PROMPT: Can you come up with an outline for an alien invasion story?

REPLY: Title: "Cosmic Clash: Invasion from Beyond"
Outline:
Introduction
Introduce the peaceful and harmonious planet Earth, teeming with diverse life forms.
Briefly establish the normalcy and tranquility of everyday life.
Mysterious Signs
Unusual celestial phenomena capture the attention of scientists and astronomers.

Strange signals and unidentified objects in space spark curiosity and speculation.

First Contact

Alien spacecraft suddenly appear in Earth's skies, causing widespread awe and panic.

Governments and world leaders attempt to establish communication and understand their intentions.

Invasion Begins

Alien invaders launch an aggressive assault, targeting major cities around the globe.

Advanced technologies and devastating weapons pose a formidable threat to human defenses.

Resistance and Survival

Introduce a group of resilient protagonists, including scientists, soldiers, and ordinary people.

Show their struggle to survive amidst the chaos and organize a resistance against the alien invaders.

Unraveling the Mystery

Uncover the aliens' motives behind the invasion, revealing their quest for Earth's resources or other hidden agendas.

Protagonists discover crucial information that may hold the key to turning the tide against the invaders.

Heroic Battles and Alliances

Epic battles ensue as human forces unite, utilizing their resilience, ingenuity, and the strength of newfound alliances.

Highlight acts of bravery and sacrifice, as well as unexpected alliances with friendly extraterrestrial beings.

Humanity's Last Stand

Protagonists embark on a daring mission to disable the alien invaders' central command or weaken their defenses.

Show the climax of the battle, where humanity's survival hangs in the balance.

Victory or Defeat

Depict the final confrontation between humans and alien invaders, revealing the outcome of the conflict.

Highlight the triumph of the human spirit, resilience, and unity in the face of overwhelming odds.

Epilogue

Show the aftermath of the invasion, with Earth rebuilding and recovering from the devastation.

Reflect on the lessons learned, the bonds formed, and the hope for a brighter future for humanity and the universe.

This is a decent outline, even if a little generic. It offers a helpful start, and you can refine it by asking ChatGPT to expand on any section of the outline, as well as by throwing your own ideas into the mix.

You'll never obtain a fully workable outline on your first attempt. You will need to dig deeper and ask more questions. Remember, ChatGPT builds on what you discussed previously in the conversation, so you can ask lots of questions without repeating the context, and it will know what you are talking about. Let's prompt ChatGPT for more detail to build a more nuanced sense of this potential world.

PROMPT: Can you suggest some examples of how the aliens show their power?

REPLY: Certainly! Here are some examples of how the alien invaders demonstrate their power in the story:

Advanced Technology: The aliens possess highly advanced technology far beyond human comprehension. They showcase this by effortlessly disabling Earth's defenses, rendering conventional weapons ineffective. They deploy energy shields that repel human attacks and deploy devastating energy beams that can obliterate entire cities.

Mind Control: Some aliens have the ability to manipulate human minds, using telepathy or mind control devices. They showcase their power by turning humans against each other, causing confusion, and sowing discord among Earth's inhabitants.

Impenetrable Force Fields: The alien invaders deploy impenetrable force fields around their ships and installations, rendering human weapons useless. This power display frustrates human military forces and reinforces the aliens' dominance.

Terrifying Biological Adaptations: Certain alien species possess menacing physical attributes, such as razor-sharp claws, venomous fangs, or the ability to camouflage themselves. They use these adaptations to overpower and intimidate human defenders, showcasing their superiority in physical combat.

Energy Manipulation: The aliens possess the ability to harness and manipulate various forms of energy. They demonstrate this power by generating destructive energy blasts that can level buildings or disable electronic systems with a mere touch.

Teleportation and Interdimensional Travel: The aliens showcase their power by swiftly teleporting across great distances or opening portals to other dimensions. This allows them to launch surprise attacks and retreat without a trace, leaving humans bewildered and outmatched.

Superhuman Strength and Speed: Some aliens possess enhanced physical attributes, such as immense strength and lightning-fast reflexes. They effortlessly overpower human resistance, displaying their superiority in physical prowess.

Massive War Machines: The alien invaders deploy colossal war machines, towering over cities and striking fear into the hearts of humans. These imposing constructs wreak havoc, demolishing buildings and decimating human defenses with ease.

Bioweapons and Genetic Manipulation: The aliens engineer deadly bioweapons or employ genetic manipulation techniques, creating monstrous creatures to serve as their minions. These abominations exhibit incredible strength, resilience, and ferocity, instilling terror among the human population.

Planetary Manipulation: The ultimate display of power comes when the aliens showcase their ability to manipulate planetary systems. They can alter weather patterns, create destructive natural disasters, or even manipulate Earth's gravitational field, causing widespread chaos and devastation.

These power displays highlight the overwhelming might of the alien invaders and serve to underline the immense challenge faced by humanity in the story.

This provides a comprehensive list of ideas we can work with. Again, you can dig deeper and ask further probing questions, if you like. Now let's ask ChatGPT to give us ideas about how humanity can fight back against the aliens.

PROMPT: Can you suggest some examples of humanity's attempts to fight back?

REPLY: Certainly! Here are some examples of humanity's attempts to fight back against the alien invaders:

Military Resistance: Earth's armed forces rally together, utilizing their weaponry and tactical expertise to engage the alien invaders in intense battles. Fighter jets engage in aerial dogfights, ground troops launch daring assaults, and naval vessels engage in high-stakes skirmishes, showing the resilience and determination of humanity's military.

Guerrilla Tactics: Recognizing the overwhelming power of the aliens, human resistance fighters employ guerrilla warfare tactics. They strike swiftly and unexpectedly, utilizing hit-and-run attacks, sabotage, and ambushes to target vulnerable points in the alien invaders' infrastructure.

Scientific Innovation: Brilliant scientists and engineers work tirelessly to develop new technologies and weapons to counter the alien threat. They analyze captured alien technology, reverse-engineer it, and devise inventive strategies, such as electromagnetic pulse devices, energy-based weaponry, or specialized suits to neutralize the aliens' advantages.

Unity and Cooperation: Recognizing the need for solidarity, humans from all walks of life set aside their differences and unite against the common enemy. Governments, organizations, and ordinary individuals collaborate, sharing information, resources, and strategies to mount a united front against the alien invaders.

Humanitarian Resistance: Civilians join the fight in unconventional ways, providing support and aid to the resistance. They establish secret safe houses, gather intelligence, and provide logistical support, contributing to the overall resistance effort.

Strategic Counterattacks: As humanity gathers valuable intelligence on the alien invaders, they identify weaknesses or vulnerabilities in their forces. Brave teams of soldiers and scientists embark on daring missions, infiltrating enemy bases or launching surgical strikes to disrupt the invaders' operations.

Psychic Resistance: Some humans possess latent psychic abilities that they learn to harness against the alien invaders. These gifted individuals use their telepathic or empathic powers to disrupt the aliens' communication, confuse their strategies, or even directly attack their minds.

Uniting with Friendly Aliens: Humanity forms alliances with benevolent extraterrestrial beings who have observed the alien invasion. These friendly aliens offer their advanced technology, knowledge, and battle-hardened skills to assist humanity in their fight against the common foe.

Last Stand Defenses: In desperate situations, humans establish fortified strongholds and underground bunkers to protect themselves from the alien onslaught. These strategic defenses provide a last line of defense, buying time for survivors and offering hope for a counteroffensive.

Exploiting Weaknesses: Through careful observation and analysis, humans identify vulnerabilities in the aliens' biology, technology, or tactics. They exploit these weaknesses, devising creative strategies to neutralize or disrupt the invaders, such as deploying special countermeasures or developing effective biological agents.

These examples illustrate humanity's determination, resourcefulness, and resilience in the face of overwhelming odds, highlighting their unwavering spirit to fight for their home planet.

Again, we are given a detailed list of ways humans can fight back against the aliens. A mixture of guerrilla tactics and scientific innovation sounds fun. Let's expand on this example one more time and ask ChatGPT to suggest how the world would be changed forever after preventing an alien invasion.

PROMPT: Can you give a few examples of how the world has changed forever after the aliens are defeated?

REPLY: Certainly! Here are a few examples of how the world is changed forever after the aliens are defeated:

Global Unity: The alien invasion serves as a catalyst for unprecedented global unity. Nations put aside their differences and work together, establishing a newfound spirit of cooperation and collaboration. The shared experience of facing a common enemy leads to the formation of international alliances and organizations committed to safeguarding Earth's future.

Technological Advancements: The remnants of alien technology left behind after the invasion offer humanity a tremendous leap forward in scientific and technological advancements. Scientists study and adapt the alien technology, leading to breakthroughs in various fields, such as energy generation, space exploration, medicine, and transportation.

Rebuilding and Reconstruction: The aftermath of the invasion prompts a massive global rebuilding effort. Cities devastated by the conflict are reconstructed with innovative architectural designs, incorporating both aesthetics and enhanced resilience against future threats. The reconstruction also provides an opportunity to implement sustainable practices and eco-friendly infrastructure.

Heightened Preparedness: The invasion serves as a stark reminder of humanity's vulnerability. Governments invest heavily in defense systems, early warning systems, and advanced surveillance technology to detect and respond to potential future threats. Preparedness becomes a priority, ensuring that humanity is better equipped to defend itself against any future incursions.

Cultural Exchange: The encounter with alien beings sparks a global curiosity about other civilizations and worlds. Cultural exchange programs, interstellar diplomacy, and academic collaborations flourish, leading to a deeper understanding and appreciation of the diversity of life in the universe. Humanity embraces a broader perspective, fostering a new era of interplanetary exploration and peaceful coexistence.

Psychological Impact: The invasion leaves a lasting psychological impact on humanity. The trauma endured during the conflict spurs an increased focus on mental health support and resilience-building. Society becomes more empathetic and understanding, promoting healing and fostering a stronger sense of community among survivors.

Environmental Awareness: The invasion serves as a

wake-up call to humanity's responsibility as caretakers of Earth. The catastrophic events witnessed during the conflict ignite a global environmental consciousness. Efforts are intensified to preserve and restore ecosystems, combat climate change, and develop sustainable practices that ensure the long-term health of the planet.

Legacy of Heroism: The brave individuals who fought against the alien invaders become revered as heroes. Monuments, memorials, and annual commemorations are established to honor their sacrifices and celebrate their unwavering spirit. Their stories inspire future generations to stand up against adversity and strive for a better world.

Interstellar Defense: With the knowledge gained from the invasion, humanity works toward establishing a robust interstellar defense network. Vigilant monitoring of space and collaborative efforts with friendly extraterrestrial allies ensure Earth's preparedness against future potential threats.

Appreciation for Life: The invasion serves as a powerful reminder of the fragility and preciousness of life. Humanity develops a renewed appreciation for the beauty, diversity, and interconnectedness of all living beings on Earth. This awareness fuels efforts to protect and preserve life in all its forms, fostering a global movement toward compassion, empathy, and sustainable coexistence.

> These changes signify a world transformed by the harrowing experience of the alien invasion, offering humanity a chance to rebuild, learn, and grow in a way that propels them toward a brighter future.

These suggestions could provide inspiration for how you portray the world, the protagonist, and the side characters in the novel after the last battle. You can dig deeper into any of these ideas by asking further probing questions.

For me, researching and brainstorming ideas is one of the killer applications of ChatGPT. If you spend the time asking increasingly detailed, probing questions, you can fire up your imagination and ignite ideas that you may not have thought of on your own.

Some people may think this is cheating, but it really does not differ from sitting down with another person and brainstorming ideas. It's just that the other person is a non-human, generative AI. In the next section, let's look at one of the more controversial uses of ChatGPT.

ChatGPT To Rephrase Text

An arena in which ChatGPT shines is in rephrasing text, which can be controversial, but I'll come to that in a moment. For now, let's look at some simple examples. In this first example, I want to rephrase a statement in the passive voice, hopefully to the active voice.

> **PROMPT**: Rephrase "The banana was eaten by the big hairy gorilla."
>
> **REPLY**: The big, hairy gorilla devoured the banana.

We wanted the active voice, which is exactly what ChatGPT delivered. Instead of the banana being eaten by the gorilla, the gorilla eats the banana. Let's now ask ChatGPT to rephrase the statement, but with a more advanced vocabulary.

> **PROMPT**: Rephrase with more advanced vocabulary.
>
> **REPLY**: The sizeable, hirsute gorilla consumed the Musa paradisiaca with fervor.

I don't think I would use this version myself as I prefer the earlier example, but ChatGPT did exactly what we asked. Remember, if you don't like an answer, you can hit the "regenerate reply" button, and it will give you another suggestion.

ChatGPT can also fix text that is partial gibberish and reinterpret it back into legible English. The example in the following prompt is tough to read, but ChatGPT makes a short work of it.

> **PROMPT**: "Th cat likef 2 jump ov3r teh big f3nc whle it hnted for b1rds"
>
> **REPLY**: The cat liked to jump over the big fence while it hunted for birds.

Anyone who has had to survive a text chat with me using a phone would be grateful for this tool. I'm terrible at typing on a phone screen. The original prompt is very hard to read, and it takes your brain a few attempts to see what is going on, but ChatGPT got there straight away. One area where this can be useful is if you have taken hastily written notes on your phone or laptop and you use ChatGPT to tidy them up.

Now, I want to talk about a more powerful way of using rephrase that has caused significant controversy. ChatGPT is good at taking a large block of text and completely rewriting it. If your first thought is that this is a powerful tool for committing plagiarism, you would be right. Using ChatGPT that way is ethically wrong; please don't do it.

Some people state that they will never touch ChatGPT for this very reason, but I think that is a mistake. A screwdriver is a flexible tool for putting up shelves or assembling flat-packed furniture, but it also makes for an effective murder weapon. That said, we don't ban screwdrivers. We trust that most people will use the screwdriver for its intended purpose, and I believe the same is true here. Rephrasing text is a powerful feature, but use it responsibly. In the following example, I take a section from a blog post I wrote called "The Punk Rock of Publishing" and use it as a source for ChatGPT to rephrase.

PROMPT: Rephrase "One of the biggest drawbacks of traditional publishing is that writers are often required to give up the lifetime publishing rights to their work. This means that if a book doesn't sell well, the writer is often unable to republish it. This can be a huge financial blow to writers, who may have spent years working on a book only to see it fail to find an audience.

With self-publishing, writers retain the rights to their work. This means that even if a book doesn't sell well initially, the writer can continue to promote and sell it, or even republish it under a different title or with different marketing. This gives writers more control over their work and the ability to make a living from their writing."

REPLY: A notable disadvantage of conventional publishing is that authors frequently have to surrender their perpetual publishing rights to their manuscripts. Consequently, if a book is not commercially successful, the author often lacks the capacity to republish it. This could potentially result in significant financial detriment for authors, who might have devoted years to crafting a book, only to find it unsuccessful in attracting readership.

In contrast, self-publishing enables authors to maintain the rights to their work. This implies that even if a book doesn't initially generate substantial sales, the author retains the opportunity to persistently market and sell it, or even republish it with a new title or different promotional strategies. This grants authors more autonomy over their work and enhances their prospects of earning a livelihood through their writing.

The result is impressive because it can take a large block of text and rewrite it and maintain its meaning, although, I feel my original version is much better. If you have a passage of text that you have written and are not happy about it, ChatGPT can be just the tool to help you out with rephrased suggestions. But make sure you only use it in your own work and not a tool for plagiarism.

To finish this section of the book, I'd like to show some examples of using ChatGPT to create outlines of existing books that you can use to help you learn about story structure.

ChatGPT To Study Book Outlines

As writers, we are always striving to learn more about our craft and the genres we like to write in. By asking ChatGPT to write outlines for existing books on the market, you can analyse their structure. It's a fantastic way to learn. However, don't use this method as an excuse to rip off other people's plots; instead, take these ideas to further your own knowledge.

I write middle-grade novels aimed at children from nine to twelve years old. For me, one of the definitive books to read and study is *Treasure Island* by Robert Lewis Stevenson. Let's ask ChatGPT to write an outline.

PROMPT: Can you write an outline for *Treasure Island* by Robert Lewis Stevenson?

REPLY: Sure, here's a basic outline for Robert Louis Stevenson's "Treasure Island":

1. Introduction:
 - The story is set in the mid-18th century at the Admiral Benbow Inn located on the English coast.
 - Jim Hawkins, the young protagonist, helps his parents run the inn.
 - A mysterious old seaman, Billy Bones, takes up lodging at the inn.

2. Rising Action:

- Billy Bones is visited by several pirates, triggering his fatal stroke.

- After Billy's death, Jim discovers a map among Billy's belongings, indicating the location of the notorious pirate Captain Flint's buried treasure.

- Jim shows the map to Squire Trelawney and Dr. Livesey, who decide to mount an expedition to find the treasure.

- They hire a ship, the Hispaniola, and its crew, including Long John Silver, a one-legged cook, who is, unbeknownst to them, a former member of Flint's crew.

3. Climax:

- On the voyage to the island, Jim overhears Silver's plan to mutiny once the treasure is found.

- Upon reaching the island, Jim encounters Ben Gunn, a marooned sailor who had been part of Flint's crew.

- Jim discovers that Silver's mutiny has begun and many loyal crew members are killed.

- Jim retrieves the Hispaniola and brings it around to a safer harbor on the island.

4. Falling Action:

- Gunn reveals that he has already found and moved Flint's treasure.

- Jim returns to the stockade, where Silver and the mutineers are in control.

- Silver, caught between the remaining mutineers and the loyal crew members, decides to side with Jim and his friends.

5. Resolution:

- The group finds the empty treasure cache and are ambushed by the remaining mutineers.

- They manage to fend off the mutineers and locate the treasure in Ben Gunn's cave.

- They return to the Hispaniola and set sail for home, leaving the remaining mutineers marooned on the island.

- Silver escapes with a part of the treasure during the journey home, but Jim is happy to be rid of him.

6. Conclusion:

- Jim, Trelawney, Livesey, and Ben Gunn return home safely with the treasure.

- Jim concludes his tale by mentioning that the rest of Flint's treasure is still on Treasure Island, but he has no desire to undertake another adventure to retrieve it."

This outline is spot on, and for one, it shows you how to write a basic high-level outline of a novel. Just by reading this, you can gain a good feel for how the story is structured, and that is helpful when learning the craft of storytelling as you can analyse how other authors structured their books. Let's dig a little deeper and ask about the main themes in the story.

PROMPT: What are the themes of *Treasure Island* by Robert Lewis Stevenson?

REPLY: Treasure Island by Robert Louis Stevenson explores several themes:

1. Coming of Age: This is a central theme in the book. The story follows Jim Hawkins' transformation from a boy to a young man. His experiences with pirates, mutiny, and the search for treasure force him to grow and mature quickly.

2. Good versus Evil: This theme is depicted through the constant battle between the moral and upright characters, such as Jim, Dr. Livesey, and Squire Trelawney, and the unscrupulous pirates led by Long John Silver.

3. Betrayal and Loyalty: Long John Silver's duplicity and the mutiny of the crew against their officers illustrate the theme of betrayal. On the other hand, the loyalty of characters like Jim, Dr. Livesey, and Captain Smollett is also highlighted.

4. Courage and Survival: Jim shows immense bravery throughout his adventure, standing up to

dangerous pirates and taking bold actions that significantly affect the story's outcome. The theme of survival is also prevalent, with characters often facing life-or-death situations.

5. Greed and its Consequences: The treasure symbolizes wealth and the greed it can inspire. The pirates' greed leads them to mutiny and eventually to their downfall. This theme serves as a moral lesson about the dangers of excessive greed.

6. The Uncertain Nature of Morality: The character of Long John Silver embodies this theme. Despite being a pirate and a mutineer, Silver is charming, intelligent, and at times, even caring, which blurs the lines between 'good' and 'evil'. He is neither entirely villainous nor entirely virtuous, adding a layer of complexity to the story's moral landscape.

Through these themes, Stevenson weaves a rich, complex narrative that continues to captivate readers of all ages.

This is quite a detailed list, and there is much to be learned from it. Themes represent the hidden layer of a story. The plot is just a mechanism to get the characters from place to place. The themes are the real story and are what give a novel an emotional edge that readers expect. Using ChatGPT to analyse themes in novels is helpful as a teaching tool to help you craft a novel with heart and emotion. Let's try another example with a fairy tale, Little Red Riding Hood.

PROMPT: Can you write an outline to Little Red Riding Hood?

REPLY: Sure, here's a basic outline for the traditional fairy tale "Little Red Riding Hood":

I. Introduction

A. Introduction of Little Red Riding Hood, a girl who always wears a red hooded cape.

B. Her mother asks her to take a basket of food to her sick grandmother.

II. Journey through the Woods

A. Little Red Riding Hood begins her journey through the woods to her grandmother's house.

B. Encounter with the Big Bad Wolf who learns about her journey.

III. The Wolf's Deception

A. The wolf tricks Little Red Riding Hood, suggesting she pick some flowers for her grandmother.

B. While she is distracted, the wolf races ahead to the grandmother's house.

IV. The Wolf's Disguise

A. The wolf arrives at the grandmother's house, eats her, and then disguises himself as her.

B. Little Red Riding Hood arrives and is tricked by the wolf's disguise.

V. The Climax

A. Little Red Riding Hood notices strange differences about her "grandmother" (the wolf).

B. The wolf reveals himself and tries to eat Little Red Riding Hood.

VI. The Rescue

A. Just in time, a huntsman passing by hears the commotion and rescues Little Red Riding Hood and her grandmother by cutting open the wolf's stomach.

VII. Conclusion

A. The grandmother and Little Red Riding Hood fill the wolf's stomach with stones, and when he awakens, he's too heavy to escape and dies.

B. Little Red Riding Hood learns the lesson not to talk to strangers or stray from her path.

This is a basic outline of the traditional version of the story. Some versions may have slight variations in events or characters. For example, in some versions, the grandmother isn't rescued, and in others, the wolf doesn't die at the end.

As with the previous example, ChatGPT offers us a fairly detailed outline of the story to study. Being able to see at a glance an outline for already existing, and popular novels is a useful tool for a novelist as it lets you easily analyse how another author has constructed their story, and a detailed outline will be much easier to read than trying to analyse the entire novel. Of course, you should still read the novels to get a feel for an author's writing style, but the outline makes for a convenient learning tool.

Digging deeper, we can ask a follow-up question about the wolf's motivation in the story. All stories are based around characters who have their own wants and needs. Wants and needs translate into the actual motivation for a characters actions, so ChatGPT will help you study the motivations of a novels characters.

PROMPT: What was the wolf's main motivation?

REPLY: In the traditional fairy tale "Little Red Riding Hood," the wolf's main motivation is hunger. He is portrayed as a cunning predator, who uses deceit and trickery to try to satisfy his appetite. His first goal is to eat Little Red Riding Hood, but when he learns about her sick grandmother, he sees an opportunity for an even bigger meal. This leads him to hatch a plan to eat both Little Red Riding Hood and her grandmother. The wolf's actions are driven purely by his predatory instincts and his desire for food.

The reply is informative, especially if you are conducting research on your antagonist for your novel. When reading a novel, it can sometimes take a while to fully understand the motivations of all the characters, but when you are planning your own novel and you want to analyse comparable books, this form of quick research is valuable.

Let's ask one last question to obtain the key themes in Little Red Riding Hood. Themes are the story beneath the story, and novels without themes can be quite empty. Like before analysing themes so you can understand how other author incorporate them is important.

PROMPT: What are the main themes in Little Red Riding Hood?

REPLY: Little Red Riding Hood" is a rich story with several underlying themes:

   1. Obedience and the Consequences of

Disobedience: Little Red Riding Hood's mother warns her to stay on the path and not to talk to strangers. Disobeying her mother's advice, the girl strays off the path and talks to the wolf, leading to dire consequences.

2. *Innocence and the Loss of Innocence*: Little Red Riding Hood is portrayed as an innocent child who is unaware of the dangers that exist in the world. Her encounter with the wolf symbolizes the loss of innocence as she becomes aware of evil and deception.

3. *Stranger Danger*: The wolf in the story can be seen as a symbol of a dangerous stranger. Little Red Riding Hood's interaction with the wolf serves as a cautionary tale about the risks of trusting strangers.

4. *Trickery and Deception*: The wolf uses deceit to achieve his goals, first by learning about Little Red Riding Hood's journey, and then by pretending to be her grandmother.

5. *The Natural Order and Survival*: The story also reflects the harsh realities of life in earlier times, when the threat of predators was a part of daily life. The wolf, as a predator, is simply trying to eat and survive.

6. *Rescue and Redemption*: Despite the grim events, the story ends on a hopeful note with the rescue of Little Red Riding Hood and her grandmother by the huntsman. This theme underscores the potential for redemption and rescue, even in bleak circumstances.

*7. **Wisdom and the Process of Learning***: Little Red Riding Hood learns a valuable lesson about obedience and the dangers of straying from the safe path, illustrating that wisdom often comes from experience, even when that experience is negative.

These themes have helped the story retain its relevance and appeal over the centuries, allowing it to be interpreted in various ways depending on cultural context and audience age.

Learning about story structure through ChatGPT's detailed answers about your favourite books and stories can be good fun. Just remember, use these tools sensibly, and don't steal plot ideas.

In the next section of this book, I will demonstrate another outstanding feature of ChatGPT for writers: helping with the marketing of your books once you release them.

TWO

ChatGPT as a Marketing Assistant

In the fast-paced, dynamic field of marketing, professionals are continually seeking innovative tools and methods to gain an edge. As AI advances, it brings with it intriguing possibilities for the marketing world. This chapter explores the potential of leveraging AI, specifically the language model ChatGPT, in marketing your books.

Crafting compelling marketing content requires a blend of creativity, strategic thinking, market understanding, and a knack for persuasive language. However, the process can be time-consuming and, at times, challenging. From ideating catchy tag lines to writing engaging ad copy or drafting persuasive sales pitches, each task demands a particular approach. How can an

AI model like ChatGPT play a role in the creative and strategic field of marketing?

In this chapter, we'll explore the myriad ways in which ChatGPT can serve as a marketing assistant, generating ideas for tag lines, helping draft preliminary ad copies, or providing variations of promotional tweets. It can save time, boost creativity, and offer a fresh perspective when you're stuck in a marketing rut.

However, as with the previous uses we've explored, it's vital to remember that ChatGPT is a tool, not a replacement for a human marketer's expertise and intuition. We'll discuss how to use it effectively, capitalising on its strengths while being aware of its limitations. The goal of this chapter is not to suggest AI can replace human-led marketing initiatives but rather to show how AI, specifically ChatGPT, can assist writers with their marketing tasks. We'll delve into various practical applications, offering real examples and insights to help you understand how you might incorporate ChatGPT into your own marketing processes.

Writing Blurbs is Hard

When we talk about writing marketing copy for a book, the main piece of text that comes to mind is the book description, often called the blurb. The book description does exactly as the name suggests. It's a description of the book and plot whose purpose is to convince the potential reader to buy the book. It's the second thing a reader is likely to engage with in a store, or online, after being attracted by the book's cover. The description is there to sell the book.

In my experience as a long-time author, writing a book description is very hard. I often joke that writing the description for my debut novel, *Diary of a Martian*, released in 2023, was harder than writing the novel itself. The book description took me around two weeks to write. It involved several drafts, soliciting feedback from peers in various writing communities, who often gave conflicting views and advice, and then sending the description to my editor. In the end, I was very pleased with the description, and it has helped me sell *Diary of a Martian*, but it was hard work. Here is the book description I landed on.

Elliot's a Martian. Although you wouldn't know it – he's just like a regular kid from Earth ... except he was born on Mars.

Life in a Martian colony can be tough for a twelve-year-old! You can't just go outside to hang out because, well, you'd suffocate and die.

Elliot lives a regular Martian life. He goes to school, plays football, and tries to avoid the mean kids. But he never gets to leave the colony buildings. That is, until he goes on a science trip where he makes a discovery that could change the course of humanity forever: a strange doorway in a volcanic cave! Who put it there? What's on the other side?

Join Elliot and his friends as their lives go from the ordinary to the extraordinary. The solar system as we know it will never be the same again.

Later in this section of the book, I will use ChatGPT to rewrite this book description and the rest of the marketing copy for the novel. At the time of writing this book on ChatGPT, I am preparing the sequel to *Diary of a Martian* for release. For the sequel's description, I went straight to ChatGPT, fed in some details about the book's plot, and then let the AI take over. I took ChatGPT's book description, did some light editing on it myself, sent it to my editor, who provided her feedback within a few hours, and then gave it to my son – who is in the target reading age – and applied some of his comments. I completed this entire process within a day, and I love the result. For reference, here is the book description that was initially written by ChatGPT, before I applied my edits.

> In this action-packed sequel to Diary of a Martian, join Elliot, Mei, and Dimitri as they find themselves in the middle of a three-thousand-year-old conspiracy.
>
> Since first contact with the Vehni, an alien race, the human colonists of New London, Mars, have been enjoying the benefits of shared Vehni technology. But when ambassadors from Earth attempt to hijack the Vehni ship in orbit, everything the colonists thought they knew about their alien allies is thrown into question.
>
> Who are the Vehni, and how did Earth's people gain the knowledge to hijack their advanced vessel? As Elliot and his two friends set out to uncover the truth behind the hijacking, a secret Vehni technology is uncovered with the power to change humanity's destiny.
>
> Rocket into an adventure full of thrilling twists and turns, where friendship and courage are put to the test.

Diary of a Martian: Soul Soldiers is perfect for readers who crave an exciting, and out-of-this-world experience.

Let's now take a deeper look at using ChatGPT to write marketing material, including cover book descriptions, log lines, tag lines, sales paragraphs, and promotional social media messages, for some example books.

ChatGPT to Write a Blurb for Diary of a Martian

For my first example, I want to use ChatGPT to have a go at rewriting the blurb for my first novel, *Diary of a Martian*. I am happy with my original blurb, but let's see what ChatGPT can come up with. I don't need to provide a full in-depth synopsis – just enough key details that I think the potential reader should know about.

PROMPT: I am writing a middle-grade children's novel about a boy called Elliot who is a fourth-generation Martian living in the New London Mars colony. Mars is a dangerous place, and kids don't go outside until they are 12. When out on a science expedition, he makes a discovery that could change the course of human existence and helps answer the question, "Are we alone in the universe?" Can you write a book description that is suitable for a middle-grade audience and is compelling enough to make the reader want to buy the book. The book is called Diary of a Martian.

REPLY: Discover the thrilling and mysterious world of Elliot, a fourth-generation Martian living in the bustling New London Mars Colony, in 'Diary of a Martian.' This captivating middle-grade novel takes readers on an unforgettable adventure through the cosmos, where the age-old question of 'Are we alone in the universe?' awaits an answer.

In the treacherous landscape of Mars, children are forbidden from venturing outside the safety of the colony until they turn twelve. But for Elliot, his twelfth birthday marks the beginning of a life-altering journey. Join him as he steps beyond the colony walls for the first time, accompanied by a team of scientists on a riveting expedition.

Along the way, Elliot stumbles upon a mysterious discovery that could not only change the course of human existence but also redefine everything we thought we knew about life in the universe. As he finds himself entangled in a web of secrets and intrigue, Elliot must summon his courage, resourcefulness, and unyielding determination to unlock the truth.

'Diary of a Martian' is an enchanting tale of friendship, discovery, and the indomitable spirit of human curiosity. Readers will be drawn into the vividly imagined world of New London, where danger and wonder lurk around every corner. This heart-pounding, cosmic adventure will leave you eagerly turning the pages, as Elliot's story unfolds and he learns that sometimes, the most extraordinary secrets are hidden in the most unexpected places.

Get ready for an out-of-this-world experience that will leave you questioning the limits of our universe and the untapped potential of the human spirit. Dive into 'Diary of a Martian' today, and let your imagination soar to the stars!

As you can see, you don't need to provide much information for ChatGPT to write a blurb. From just a handful of details, it has come back with an extensive book description.

As relevant as this description is, however, there is one issue: it's far too long. My book is targeted to readers in the middle-grade category, ages nine to twelve years old. Let's ask ChatGPT to write a shorter and more age-appropriate version.

PROMPT: Can you write a shorter version suitable for readers aged 10-12?

REPLY: Join Elliot, a fourth-generation Martian, as he embarks on a thrilling adventure in 'Diary of a Martian.' When Elliot turns twelve, he steps outside the New London Mars Colony for the first time, eager to explore the mysterious red planet.

On a daring science expedition, Elliot stumbles upon a secret that could change everything we know about life in the universe. With danger and wonder around every corner, Elliot must use his courage and determination to uncover the truth.

Dive into this exciting, cosmic adventure and find out if we are truly alone in the universe. Get ready to explore the stars with 'Diary of a Martian' today!

This version is a suitable length, and it reads well, based on the facts I provided. It will also likely sell my book better than the first one. When you sell a book on online stores like Amazon, you need to treat Amazon for what it is: a massive search engine. This means you want your book to appear in the search results for relevant readers. To do this, you must ensure that your book title and description include relevant keywords. Amazon is a search engine, just like Google, so search engine optimisation is important. Let's say I have identified the following series of keywords that I want to include: Martian, Mars, New London, exploration, science fiction, action and adventure. Let's now ask ChatGPT to have another go at the blurb using my keywords.

PROMPT: Can you include the keywords: Martian, Mars, New London, Exploration, Science Fiction, Action and Adventure?

REPLY: Embark on a thrilling **Martian** adventure with 'Diary of a **Martian**,' an exciting science fiction tale set in the **New London** Mars Colony. Elliot, a fourth-generation **Martian**, steps outside the colony walls for the first time on his twelfth birthday, eager to explore the wonders of **Mars**.

Join Elliot as he uncovers a hidden secret that could change our understanding of life in the universe. This **action**-packed, cosmic **exploration** story will captivate readers aged 10-12 as they follow Elliot's journey filled with danger, discovery, and friendship.

Grab your space gear and get ready for an unforgettable ride through **Mars** and beyond in 'Diary of a **Martian**,' the ultimate **exploration** and **adventure** story for young readers!

In this version of the blurb, ChatGPT has integrated all my chosen keywords, which I have highlighted.

Next, I want to ask ChatGPT to write a sales paragraph. This paragraph is intended to convince the potential reader to purchase your book. The book's description tells the reader what the book is about, whereas the sales paragraph tries to convert them to buying the book. When selling the book in a store like Amazon, the product description section of your sales page would include the book description, followed by the sales paragraph. As I am in the same ChatGPT session, the AI already knows about my book and book description, so I can simply ask it to write the sales paragraph.

PROMPT: Can you write a sales paragraph to encourage people to start reading the book?

REPLY: Don't miss out on the chance to join Elliot, a fearless young Martian, as he embarks on a breathtaking journey in 'Diary of a Martian.' Bursting with excitement, action, and adventure, this science fiction tale set in the New London Mars Colony is a must-read for young explorers aged 10-12. Unravel the mysteries of the universe alongside Elliot and discover the secrets hidden within the red planet. If you're ready for a thrilling, out-of-this-world experience that will ignite your imagination and leave you eagerly turning the pages, start reading 'Diary of a Martian' today! The cosmos is waiting for you – are you ready to answer the call?

This first attempt isn't bad, but I feel it's too long, so I can ask ChatGPT to write a shorter version with more of a sales focus.

> **PROMPT**: Can you write a shorter version, but with a sales focus?
>
> **REPLY**: Get ready for an exhilarating adventure in 'Diary of a Martian'! Follow young Elliot as he uncovers Mars' hidden secrets in this action-packed science fiction tale. Perfect for 10-12-year-olds, this gripping story will spark their imagination and leave them eager for more. Embark on this cosmic journey today – 'Diary of a Martian' awaits!

This version is much better. It's shorter and more to the point. Finally, I want to make one more tweak and not reference the age group (ten- to twelve-year-olds) as although the book is primarily intended for middle graders, I know I have many readers of all ages.

PROMPT: Can you write it again but not mention 10-12 year olds? The book is suitable for younger and older readers alike.

REPLY: Embark on an exhilarating adventure with 'Diary of a Martian'! Join young Elliot as he uncovers Mars' hidden secrets in this action-packed science fiction tale. Perfect for readers of all ages, this captivating story will ignite imaginations and leave them craving more. Don't wait – dive into the cosmic journey of 'Diary of a Martian' today!

Now that I have a workable book description and sales paragraph, let's look at the book's log lines and tag lines. A log line is a brief, one- or two-sentence summary that captures the essence of a book's plot or central theme. It hooks the reader's interest and gives them a clear, concise understanding of what the book is about. Log lines are often used in marketing materials, pitches to publishers, or on the back cover of the book to engage potential readers quickly. A good log line typically includes the protagonist, their goal, and the main conflict or challenge they must overcome. Let's get started by asking ChatGPT to write a few examples based on what it already knows about the book.

PROMPT: Can you write a series of loglines for the book?

REPLY: 1. Unraveling Mars' mysteries: Elliot's daring quest to uncover the truth about life in the universe.

2. Secrets on the red planet: A young Martian's discovery that could change the course of human existence.

3. The cosmic adventure begins: Join Elliot as he explores the uncharted wonders of Mars in 'Diary of a Martian.'

4. Courage, friendship, and the unknown: Elliot's journey to unlock the hidden secrets of Mars.

5. Beyond the colony walls: A thrilling Martian adventure awaits Elliot as he uncovers the truth about our place in the universe.

These are great starting suggestions. I quite like number 2, "Secrets on the red planet: A young Martian's discovery that could change the course of human existence." If none of the suggestions appeal to you, just regenerate the response for more options.

Let's now ask ChatGPT for some tag lines. A tag line is a catchy and memorable phrase that encapsulates the tone, theme, or premise of the book. It is designed to intrigue and entice potential readers, generating curiosity about the book's content. Unlike a log line, which summarises the plot, a tag line more often conveys the book's mood or key theme in a compelling way. Tag lines are frequently used in marketing materials, on the book cover, or in promotional campaigns to capture attention and interest. Let's see what ChatGPT comes up with.

PROMPT: Can you write a series of taglines for the book?

REPLY: 1. Uncover the secrets of Mars, one diary entry at a time.

2. A cosmic adventure awaits in the pages of 'Diary of a Martian.'

3. Explore the red planet's mysteries with Elliot – the universe holds more than you know.

4. Beyond the stars lies the truth: Discover what's hidden in 'Diary of a Martian.'

5. Where courage meets curiosity: Elliot's quest to redefine humanity's place in the cosmos.

My personal favourite here is number 5, "Where courage meets curiosity: Elliot's quest to redefine humanity's place in the cosmos." Again, if you don't like the suggestions, just regenerate the response until you find something that works for you. We now have an excellent set of drafts for the marketing texts for the book: a book description, sales paragraph, log lines and tag lines. Let's turn to promotional tweets.

PROMPT: Can you write a series of tweets to promote the book?

REPLY: 1. 🚀 Blast off on an incredible journey with 'Diary of a Martian'! Join Elliot as he unveils the hidden secrets of Mars. Get your copy today! #DiaryOfAMartian #MarsAdventure

2. 🪐 Unravel the mysteries of the universe in 'Diary of a Martian.' Follow Elliot's thrilling Martian adventure and see where it leads! #RedPlanetSecrets #DiaryOfAMartian

3. 🔭 Curious about life beyond Earth? Dive into the pages of 'Diary of a Martian' and explore the cosmos with Elliot, a fourth-generation Martian. Don't miss out! #CosmicMystery #DiaryOfAMartian

4. 📘 Adventure, friendship, and discovery – 'Diary of a Martian' has it all! Join Elliot as he unlocks the secrets of Mars and redefines our place in the universe. #MarsAdventure #DiaryOfAMartian

5. Are we truly alone in the universe? Find out in 'Diary of a Martian,' where Elliot's journey through Mars will leave you questioning everything you thought you knew. #RedPlanetRevelations #DiaryOfAMartian

I like that ChatGPT's suggested tweets include emojis as they suit Twitter. However, you don't just have to use these for Twitter; they make excellent ad copy for use with Facebook ads. Now that I have covered writing the marketing materials for one of my own books, let's try another example by bringing back Little Red Riding Hood.

ChatGPT to Write a Blurb for Little Red Riding Hood

We can start with a simple request to write the blurb for Little Red Riding Hood. We don't need to tell ChatGPT any details about the plot as the fairy tale is well known, so the story is already included in the model's training data.

PROMPT: Can you write a book blurb for the story little red riding hood?

REPLY: Title: Scarlet Trails: A Tale of Little Red Riding Hood

In the enchanted heart of a mystical forest lies a story of innocence, deception, and courage. Journey through the pages of 'Scarlet Trails: A Tale of Little Red Riding Hood,' as we follow the fearless young girl with a crimson cloak on a mission to deliver a basket of goodies to her ailing grandmother.

Venture deep into the woods with Little Red Riding Hood as she encounters a charming yet deceitful stranger—a wolf with sinister intentions. As the cunning creature hatches a devious plan to prey on her grandmother, Little Red Riding Hood must rely on her intuition, bravery, and the wisdom of forest friends to unveil the deceit and save her beloved granny.

Beneath the canopy of ancient trees, 'Scarlet Trails' weaves a classic tale of love, family, and the power of innocence. This captivating retelling of the timeless folktale will have readers young and old spellbound, reminding us all that even in the darkest woods, the light of courage and hope can prevail.

I think we can agree that this blurb is pretty good and is instantly recognisable as Little Red Riding Hood, while also doing something new and interesting with the story.

A fantastic feature of ChatGPT is that it can instantly alter the style of a text. To test this, I asked ChatGPT to rewrite the blurb, but this time changing the style to that of a regency romance.

PROMPT: Can you rewrite in the style of a regency romance.

REPLY: Title: The Crimson Cloak: A Regency Rendition of Little Red Riding Hood

In the genteel world of Regency England, where manners and propriety reign supreme, a young lady draped in a striking crimson cloak embarks on a journey that will challenge the very essence of her upbringing. 'The Crimson Cloak: A Regency Rendition of Little Red Riding Hood' is a tale of romance, intrigue, and the unwavering spirit of a young heroine.

Accompany Miss Redelia Hood as she navigates the forested path to her dear grandmother's estate, bearing a basket filled with delicacies and a heart brimming with familial devotion. Amidst the labyrinth of towering trees and winding trails, Redelia encounters the enigmatic and charming Lord Wolfington, a gentleman with secrets as dark as the woods themselves.

As Lord Wolfington endeavors to outwit Redelia and her grandmother in a high-stakes game of deception, our heroine must rely on her intuition, the guidance of her woodland allies, and the stirrings of a newfound love to unmask the truth and protect her family.

'The Crimson Cloak' is a Regency romance that breathes new life into the classic tale of Little Red Riding Hood, weaving a story of courage, passion, and the unwavering power of a young woman's heart. Immerse yourself in this enchanting journey, as love and loyalty triumph over duplicity in the captivating world of Regency England.

Again, ChatGPT has produced a very competent description but this time in the style of a regency romance, making an impressive change in the overall style and tone of the first blurb. Let's push ChatGPT further and this time go in the opposite stylistic direction by choosing to rewrite the description as a heart-stopping thriller and action adventure.

> **PROMPT**: Can you rewrite in the style of a heart-stopping thriller and action adventure?
>
> **REPLY**: Title: Red Alert: A High-Stakes Pursuit of Little Red Riding Hood
>
> In a world where danger lurks around every corner and the shadows conceal deadly secrets, 'Red Alert: A High-Stakes Pursuit of Little Red Riding Hood' thrusts readers into a pulse-pounding, action-packed adventure that will leave you breathless.
>
> Young and fearless, Scarlett 'Red' Hood is tasked with the perilous mission to deliver a top-secret parcel to her ailing grandmother. As she journeys deep into the heart of the treacherous forest, Red finds herself entangled in a sinister web of deceit and terror, orchestrated by a ruthless, enigmatic adversary—the cunning and vicious Alpha Wolf.
>
> With time running out and the fate of her family

hanging in the balance, Red must rely on her instincts, combat skills, and the help of unlikely allies to outmanoeuvre her cunning foe. The chase is on, as Red and Alpha Wolf engage in a high-stakes game of cat and mouse that will test the limits of courage, loyalty, and survival.

'Red Alert' is a heart-stopping thriller and action-adventure that takes the timeless tale of Little Red Riding Hood to new, adrenaline-fuelled heights. Strap in and hold on tight as you join Red on an unforgettable journey, where the stakes have never been higher, and the line between hunter and hunted is razor-thin.

Again, ChatGPT produces an excellent attempt at an action adventure version of Little Red Riding Hood. I can almost see the movie version in the cinemas. It's easy to imagine Little Red Riding Hood working well as a gothic horror, so let's get ChatGPT to try another version. This time, I ask it to produce a shorter version as the previous descriptions were quite long.

PROMPT: Can you rewrite a shorter version in the style of a very scary gothic horror?

REPLY: Title: Crimson Shadows: The Dark Chronicles of Little Red Riding Hood

Dare to step into the eerie realm of 'Crimson Shadows: The Dark Chronicles of Little Red Riding Hood,' where the sinister reaches of the gothic forest conceal unspeakable horrors. As young Red ventures into the ominous woods to reach her ailing grandmother, she becomes ensnared in the twisted machinations of a malevolent force—the bloodthirsty, shape-shifting Wolf.

In this chilling tale of dread and darkness, Red's courage and resolve will be put to the ultimate test as she confronts the sinister creature lurking beneath the moonlit canopy. Prepare for a spine-tingling, nightmarish journey, where the line between reality and terror blurs, and only the most steadfast hearts can withstand the torment of 'Crimson Shadows.'

I think this works well as a near-final book description. At this stage, I would always perform a hand edit and then solicit feedback from readers and an editor, but for raw output from ChatGPT, it provides excellent material to work with.

Now we have a book description, let's ask ChatGPT to write the sales paragraph, a few log lines and tag lines, and social media material. You can see my prompts and ChatGPT's replies for all this content below.

PROMPT: Can you write a short sales paragraph to encourage people to buy the book?

REPLY: Dive into the gripping pages of "Crimson Shadows: The Dark Chronicles of Little Red Riding Hood" and embark on a spine-chilling journey that will leave you breathless. This haunting reimagining of the classic tale is filled with unexpected twists, heart-pounding suspense, and terrifying encounters that will keep you on the edge of your seat. A must-read for fans of gothic horror, "Crimson Shadows" is an unforgettable experience that you won't be able to put down. Order your copy now and prepare to be captivated by the eerie, spellbinding world that awaits you within its pages.

PROMPT: Can you write a series of loglines for the book?

REPLY: 1. In the shadowy depths of a gothic forest, a young girl's quest to save her grandmother unearths unspeakable horrors and a shape-shifting nemesis.

2. As darkness descends, Red must confront the sinister Wolf lurking among the twisted branches, in a chilling battle for survival that will change them both forever.

3. Bloodcurdling secrets emerge when Red ventures into the nightmarish woods, where terror awaits and only the bravest souls can withstand the torment of 'Crimson Shadows.'

4. Red's courage is put to the ultimate test as she delves into a world of darkness and dread, uncovering the truth behind the malevolent force haunting her family.

5. In a realm where reality and terror blur, Red's race against time to save her grandmother plunges her into a twisted, heart-pounding nightmare that will leave readers breathless.

PROMPT: Can you write a series of taglines for the book?

REPLY: 1. Fear the shadows, embrace the darkness.

2. A chilling journey through the heart of terror.

3. When night falls, the hunt begins.

4. Unravel the sinister secrets hidden beneath the crimson cloak.

5. One girl, one forest, an unspeakable nightmare.

6. In the depths of darkness, a crimson trail of terror awaits.

7. A tale of courage in the face of unspeakable horrors.

8. Beyond the shadows, only the fearless will survive.

9. The twisted path to salvation lies within the 'Crimson Shadows.'

10. Confront the darkness, uncover the truth, and face your fears.

Now, let's prepare the promotional tweets and Facebook ad copy to promote the book and encourage people to click a link onto a store, such as Amazon, to purchase the book.

PROMPT: Can you write a series of tweets to promote the book?

REPLY: 1. 🌲 Unravel the chilling secrets within the gothic forest. 'Crimson Shadows: The Dark Chronicles of Little Red Riding Hood' is a spine-tingling horror you won't be able to put down! Get your copy now! 🔗 #CrimsonShadows #GothicHorror

2. 💀🌳 Dive into a world of darkness and terror with 'Crimson Shadows,' where Red confronts unspeakable horrors lurking beneath the twisted branches. A must-read for horror fans! 🔗 #CrimsonShadows #RedsNightmare

3. 💧🌳 Are you brave enough to face the malevolent force haunting Red's family? Embark on a heart-pounding journey with 'Crimson Shadows: The Dark Chronicles of Little Red Riding Hood.' Get your copy today! 🔗 #CrimsonShadows #GothicTerror

4. ⏳🌳 Time is running out for Red as she ventures into the nightmarish woods to save her grandmother. Experience the torment of 'Crimson Shadows' and uncover the truth behind the terrifying shape-shifting Wolf. 🔗 #CrimsonShadows #FearTheWolf

5. ●💧 Prepare to be captivated by the eerie, spellbinding world of 'Crimson Shadows.' One girl, one forest, an unspeakable nightmare. Order your copy now and embark on a chilling adventure you'll never forget! 🔗 #CrimsonShadows #GothicHorrorAdventure

With ad copy, you don't have to just pick one version, which is good news when you have so many great options! Over time, you can run a campaign and use all these tweets to broadcast the message over social media and in your paid ad campaigns.

Writing marketing text is something that strikes fear into many writers. While it's still considered writing, it is a different skill to writing a novel. Writing marketing text is something I have always struggled with, so using a tool like ChatGPT assist with the marketing of my books has been a revelation. No matter how you feel about using artificial intelligence to assist with writing a novel, I urge writers to try it when trying to promote their own books.

ChatGPT doesn't always get it right, and what it produces require the human touch to improve it. But it will get you into a position where you have competent versions of your marketing text to improve on.

THREE

In Conclusion: Embracing the Future of Writing with ChatGPT

As we draw this explorative journey to a close, it's time to reflect on the ground we've covered and the insights we've gleaned about using ChatGPT as an assistant for writers and marketers.

Throughout this book, we've navigated the terrain of AI, focusing on OpenAI's language model, ChatGPT. We've unpacked the mechanics of how it works, providing an accessible explanation of this fascinating technology. We touched upon the different versions of the model, highlighting the iterative advancements and capabilities each version brought to the table.

We've also tackled the important topic of ethics, considering the implications of generative AI, like ChatGPT, in the writing world. We discussed the essential need for fact-checking and not taking the information generated by AI at face value.

An integral part of our discussion was about the applications of ChatGPT for writers and marketers. We explored how ChatGPT could serve as an innovative tool for brainstorming, text generation, and even as a thesaurus or research assistant. The practical uses, examples, and insights provided aimed to illustrate how AI can be a valuable aid in the creative process, whether you're crafting a novel, a poem, a screenplay, or a compelling piece of marketing copy.

Despite the potential benefits, we acknowledged the apprehensions and reservations many might have about this new technology. It's natural to fear what we don't understand or what seems to threaten the status quo. Drawing parallels with past technological advancements like the Industrial Revolution, computers, or photography, we highlighted how innovation, initially feared, eventually led to progress and new opportunities.

However, it's important to remember that these tools, including ChatGPT, aren't here to replace humans. They're designed to assist us and augment our abilities. As a writer or marketer, your creativity, insights, unique voice, and intuition are irreplaceable and invaluable. AI is a tool that can help make your process more efficient or provide a fresh perspective when you need it.

Whether you're an AI enthusiast or a sceptic, it's

important to understand what these tools can do. They are becoming increasingly integrated into our world, and understanding them enables us to make informed decisions. Even if you don't choose to use AI in your writing or marketing process, knowing its capabilities allows you to stay updated with the evolving landscape.

The intersection of technology and creativity is a space filled with potential. As we move forward, it's exciting to imagine how tools like ChatGPT could shape the future of writing and marketing. Remember, the aim is not to replace the human touch but to enhance it — to give you more tools to express your creativity, tell your stories, and reach your audience.

So, as we close this book, let's look towards the future with open minds, ready to explore, ready to adapt, and ready to embrace the potential that tools like ChatGPT present. After all, the written word is our realm, and any tool that aids us in our journey is worth understanding.

Please Leave a Review

Thank you for purchasing this book and supporting an independent writer.

If you enjoyed *Using ChatGPT as a Writer's Assistant*, I would be very grateful if you could leave a rating and review at the store you bought the book.

Reviews are very helpful to authors.

Also by stephen haunts

On Writing Your First Novel: The Journey of a Wannabe Novelist is a guide from Stephen Haunts, an experienced nonfiction author turned novelist, exploring the in-depth journey of crafting a debut novel and preparing it for publication, offering first-time authors indispensable advice to navigate the world of novel-writing.

Also by stephen haunts

Between football games and bullies, living on Mars seems a lot like living on Earth. That is, until twelve-year-old Elliot makes a discovery that may hold the key to one of humanity's biggest questions: Are we alone in the universe?

www.ingramcontent.com/pod-product-compliance
Lightning Source LLC
Chambersburg PA
CBHW042116100526
44587CB00025B/4069